D0064268

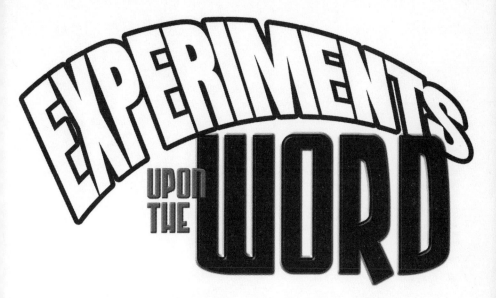

101 Object Lessons
for Latter-day Saints

• Susan Luke •

Covenant Communications, Inc.

Cover image Val Bagley © 2007

Cover design copyrighted 2007 by Covenant Communications, Inc.

Published by Covenant Communications, Inc.
American Fork, Utah

Printed in Canada
First Printing: August 2007

13 12 11 10 09 08 07   10 9 8 7 6 5 4 3 2 1

ISBN 978-1-59811-432-4

To my family for all of their love and support

CONTENTS

INTRODUCTION

My own experience has shown me that no matter what the age of the students being taught, object lessons are of great value. Whether you're trying to hold the attention of the very young, keep teenagers awake, or teach a basic gospel principle to "seasoned" members by putting a new twist on it, object lessons get the job done. Christ, the greatest teacher of all, used everyday objects all the time when teaching gospel principles. A lesson that is seen, and not just heard, can have a lasting effect on those being taught. Your students may not remember every lesson they hear, but you can bet they will remember every lesson they see. After one particular lesson, some of the teenagers in a class I was teaching were inspired to go home and present the same object lesson to their families. Now, that's a lesson they'll remember! As with anything, practice makes perfect. When you find an experiment that will help you get the point across, practice it at home until you get it just right. You want the experiment to be successful so that the lesson will be memorable. Many of the experiments in this book have more than one gospel application. You may even think of other gospel principles that can be taught with the various experiments. Check the index to see which experiments you might use to teach a particular gospel principle. However you decide to use them, have fun experimenting upon the word!

ADVERSITY BRINGS BLESSINGS

"For after much tribulation come the blessings." D&C 58:4

THINGS YOU WILL NEED
Backpack
Several heavy objects
Gift-wrapping supplies

EXPERIMENT

Wrap the various objects with gift wrap and label each gift with a different trial and possible blessing that could result from the trial. Place the wrapped objects in the backpack. Allow a class member to place the pack on their back to demonstrate its heaviness. At the appropriate time, take the gifts from the pack one at a time, discussing each trial and its corresponding blessing.

GOSPEL APPLICATION

As you allow a class member to place the pack on their back, explain that trials and tribulations can sometimes be heavy burdens to carry. We can endure our trials more easily if we remember that often they bring blessings from Heavenly Father. D&C 58:4 states, "For after much tribulation come the blessings." After having the class member carry the heavy pack, remove the "trials" one at a time, discussing the blessing that each one brings.

Note: If you wish, the gifts could contain treats or rewards that could be unwrapped and shared in class.

ALL THINGS ARE POSSIBLE

". . . all things are possible to him that believeth." Mark 9:23

THINGS YOU WILL NEED
   Large index card
   Scissors

EXPERIMENT
   Fold the index card in half from top to bottom. Cut a long notch from the folded side as shown by the dashed lines. Make 7 or 9 deep cuts (must be an odd number), alternating with one cut starting on the folded side of the card and the other starting at the other side. Unfold the card to reveal a large loop of paper large enough to step through.

GOSPEL APPLICATION
   Ask a volunteer to come forward and give them the large index card. Ask if they think it's possible to stretch the index card large enough, without tearing it, that they could step through it. After the volunteer determines it to be an impossible task, demonstrate how it is possible by cutting the card the proper way. Explain that even though we may not always understand how God can accomplish things, we must trust in Him and believe that "all things are possible to him that believeth."

ANCHORED TO THE GOSPEL

"Lay hold upon the gospel of Christ, which shall be set before you." Mormon 7:8

THINGS YOU WILL NEED
Rope (approx. 20')
Access to a tree

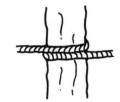

EXPERIMENT

Ask three people to hold one end of the rope, and one person to hold the other end. At your signal, have each side pull on the rope. It is easy for the side with three to pull the rope from the one (or to at least pull it in their direction.) Now wrap the rope once around the trunk of a tree. At your signal, have each side pull again. The three people can no longer pull the rope from the one.

GOSPEL APPLICATION

The tree represents the gospel. When we anchor ourselves to the gospel, things such as peace and happiness cannot easily be pulled from us.

ADDITIONAL APPLICATIONS

Commitment to the Lord—Without a true commitment to serve the Lord, the adversary can easily pull us around. But when we commit ourselves to serving the Lord, we are given strength and support to resist the tuggings of the adversary and his followers.

Negative Peer Pressure—With the support of a loving family and Church leaders and a testimony of Jesus Christ, we can resist the pull of negative peer pressure.

ANCHORED TO THE SCRIPTURES

"Whoso [will] hearken unto the word of God, and [will] hold fast unto it, they [will] never perish." 1 Nephi 15:24

THINGS YOU WILL NEED
Vacuum cleaner
Scriptures
Paper people (see pattern)
Clear tape
Strips of paper labeled with worldly things, such as unclean movies, immodest fashions, drugs and alcohol, etc.

EXPERIMENT
Cut out several paper people following the pattern. Fold back along the dotted line so the paper people will stand freely. Place several of the people on a table. Place the rest of the people on top of the scriptures with their feet taped securely to the scriptures. At the appropriate time in the demonstration, vacuum up the paper people. Those that are not anchored to the scriptures will be "sucked into the world."

GOSPEL APPLICATION
Nephi taught his brothers that "whoso would hearken unto the word of God, and would hold fast unto it, they would never perish; neither could the temptations and the fiery darts of the adversary overpower them unto blindness, to lead them away to destruction" (1 Nephi 15:24). The scriptures are the word of God. We can anchor ourselves firmly to the scriptures through diligent study of and obedience to the commandments contained therein. During the demonstration, discuss the prepared labels and tape them to the vacuum cleaner (the world). Turn on the vacuum. Run the hose over the people on

5

the table to show how easy it is for people to be deceived and sucked into the world if they are not properly anchored. Now run the hose over the rest of the people. They are secure because they are anchored to the scriptures.

ARMOR OF GOD

"Put on the whole armour of God, that ye may be able to stand against the wiles of the devil." Ephesians 6:11

THINGS YOU WILL NEED
Two oranges
Bowl of water

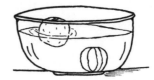

EXPERIMENT

Float the oranges in the bowl of water. Remove one of the oranges from the water and peel the skin away. Place the peeled orange into the water. It will now sink to the bottom of the bowl.

GOSPEL APPLICATION

We learn from Ephesians 6:11–18 that we are to put on the whole armor of God, which includes truth, righteousness, peace, faith, salvation, and His word. When we put on the whole armor of God through righteous living and obedience to His commandments, we protect ourselves from the "fiery darts of the wicked" (Ephesians 6:16). Just as the skin of the orange provides protection and gives the orange the ability to float atop the water, the armor of God gives us the ability to live above the wicked things of this world. Without its protection, we sink.

ADDITIONAL APPLICATION

Temptation—The scriptures warn us several times not to give in to temptations. Satan and his followers would like nothing better than to deceive us and trick us into sin. As long as we live righteously, we have the strength to overpower him. This is demonstrated by the oranges floating on the water. But when we allow ourselves to be tempted by Satan, little by little

7

he peels away our strength and protection. Eventually he has us in a completely weakened state—one where we sink into despair and hopelessness. This is demonstrated as you gradually peel away the skin of the orange. You may choose to place the orange into the water at different stages, showing how Satan works on us a little at a time. Every time we give in, we allow ourselves to sink a little more. Eventually, all protection is peeled away and we are left to sink.

ASK OF GOD

"If any of you lack wisdom, let him ask of God . . . and it shall be given him." James 1:5

THINGS YOU WILL NEED
Clear glass of water
An 8" piece of string
Salt shaker
Ice cube

EXPERIMENT

Place the ice cube in the glass of water and have a volunteer come forward and use the string to try to lift the ice cube from the water. After the volunteer gives up, wet the end of the string with water and lay it on top of the ice cube. Sprinkle salt on top of the string as well as on the area around it. After a minute or so, the string will freeze to the ice cube and you will be able to lift it from the water.

GOSPEL APPLICATION

Discuss with the class that some problems we face in life are hard to solve on our own. Demonstrate this by challenging a class member to come forward and try to remove the ice cube from the water by using only the string. As the volunteer unsuccessfully tries different ways to lift the ice cube from the water, explain that we can try to solve the problems by ourselves, but will soon find that we are just wasting time. We need the assistance of our Heavenly Father. In James 1:5, we learn that if we are lacking in wisdom we can ask of God, in faith, and receive answers. Through prayer, we ask God to help us find answers to our problems. Wet the end of the string with water and place it on the ice cube. Sprinkle the salt on the string as well as on the area around it. While you are waiting for the string to freeze to the ice cube, have the class turn to Hebrews 11:6. We learn from this scripture that "God . . . is a rewarder of them that diligently seek him." He will reward us with the answers we seek if we truly have faith in Him. Demonstrate this by success-fully lifting the ice cube from the water.

ADDITIONAL APPLICATION

Endure to the End—1 Nephi 13:37 states, ". . . and if they endure unto the end they shall be lifted up at the last day, and shall be saved in the everlasting kingdom of the Lamb." Have two or three volunteers come forward and give them each a string and a glass of water containing an ice cube. Ask them to try to remove the ice cube from the water by using the string. After they have tried unsuccessfully, tell them there is a way this can be done, but if they want to be successful, they need to endure to the end. Assign students to read aloud the following scriptures: Matthew 5:13, Ezekiel 43:24, 3 Nephi 12:13, and D&C 101:39. Ask what all of the scriptures have in common. (Salt.) Bring out the salt shaker and complete the experiment. After waiting a minute or so, have someone read 1 Nephi 13:37 aloud as your volunteers successfully lift their ice cubes from the water.

THE ATONEMENT–1

"If we walk in the light . . . the blood of Jesus Christ his Son cleanseth us from all sin." 1 John 1:7

THINGS YOU WILL NEED
Clear glass jar
1/4 cup vinegar
A pinch of salt
10 to 20 copper pennies
Steel nail
Scouring powder

EXPERIMENT

Pour the vinegar and salt into the jar. Add the pennies and let the jar stand for a few minutes. Clean the iron nail with the scouring powder and rinse thoroughly. Drop the clean nail into the vinegar with the pennies and let sit for about fifteen minutes while you continue the lesson. When the experiment is complete, the pennies will be clean and the nail will be covered with copper.

GOSPEL APPLICATION

We learn from 1 John 1:7 that through the blood of Jesus Christ we can be cleansed from our sins. The tarnished pennies represent our sinful state. The nail represents the suffering the Savior endured to bring to pass atonement for mankind. When we partake of the Atonement through sincere repentance (Mosiah 26:29–30), we can be cleansed and forgiven of our sins. Just as the nail took the tarnish from the pennies, Christ took upon Himself the burden of our sins so that if we repent, we won't have to suffer for them.

THE ATONEMENT—2

"There must be an atonement made, or else all mankind must unavoidably perish." Alma 34:9

THINGS YOU WILL NEED
Slightly scorched white cotton cloth
Clean white cotton cloth
Hydrogen peroxide
Iron

EXPERIMENT
Moisten the scorched cloth with the hydrogen peroxide. Place the clean cloth over the moistened cloth and iron until dry. The scorch will be gone.

GOSPEL APPLICATION
When a piece of clothing gets scorched, often it is considered ruined and is thrown out. Sin can ruin our lives and cause us to be cast out eternally from Heavenly Father's presence. Through the Atonement, our lives can be cleansed, giving us hope for a clean, bright eternal life.

ADDITIONAL APPLICATION
Resurrection—We learn from Alma 11:43–45 that through the resurrection "every thing shall be restored to its perfect frame, as it is now, or in the body." Demonstrate this by removing the scorch from the cloth and restoring it to its "perfect frame."

AVOID EVIL INFLUENCES

"If sinners entice thee, consent thou not." Proverbs 1:10

THINGS YOU WILL NEED
Glass of water
Teaspoon of salt
Parchment paper
Rubber band
Dish containing water
Food coloring

EXPERIMENT
Dissolve the teaspoon of salt in the glass of water and cover tightly with the parchment paper. Secure with the rubber band. Add several drops of food coloring to the water in the dish. Place the glass upside down in the dish. Eventually, the water in the glass will be colored also.

GOSPEL APPLICATION
Often people think they are immune to the influence of evil, even when it is all around them. Paul warns in Romans 16:17, "Now I beseech you, brethren, mark them which cause divisions and offences contrary to the doctrine which ye have learned; and avoid them." 1 Thessalonians 5:22 states, "Abstain from all appearance of evil." We cannot deceive ourselves and think we are always strong enough to resist the many temptations the adversary throws at us. We cannot be surrounded by evil without it having some kind of effect on us. Demonstrate this by showing how the water in the glass is affected by the colored water in the dish—even though it is supposedly protected by the parchment paper.

BAPTISM

"Repent, and be baptized every one of you in the name of Jesus Christ for the remission of sins." Acts 2:38

THINGS YOU WILL NEED
Blotting paper (found in art supply stores)
Paper clip
Water
Two clear drinking glasses
Spoon
Sand

EXPERIMENT
Make a filter from the blotting paper by cutting a circle approximately 5" in diameter. Make a straight cut from the outside of the circle to the center. Overlap the cut edges (forming a cone) and fasten with a paper clip. Set the filter aside. To begin the experiment, pour some clean water into one of the glasses. Place about one teaspoon of sand into the water and stir. Now place the cone filter in the other glass and slowly pour the sandy water through the filter. The sand should remain in the filter, leaving the water clean once again.

GOSPEL APPLICATION
The fourth Article of Faith teaches us that after we have faith in Jesus Christ, we must repent and be baptized by immersion for the remission of sins. Although each of us begins mortal life clean and pure, we will all make mistakes and thereby become unclean. Through sincere repentance and baptism by immersion, our sins can be "filtered" from our lives and we can become clean once more.

ADDITIONAL APPLICATION

Clean Living—Stir one teaspoon of sand into the water for each worldly influence the class can name. Some suggestions may be R-rated movies, immodest fashions, and vulgar language. The water becomes polluted and impure. Ask a volunteer if they would like a drink of the water. Of course not! But, how many of these wordly influences are we allowing to enter our minds and bodies each day? Pour the polluted water into the clean glass through the filter. Just as we filter the sand from the water, we need to filter the bad of the world so that only the good influences us. We accomplish that by following God's commandments and counsel. If we follow the plan that God has given us, we will learn to "Set our affection on things above, not on things on the earth" (Colossians 3:2).

BEAR ONE ANOTHER'S BURDENS

"Bear ye one another's burdens, and so fulfil the law of Christ."
Galatians 6:2

THINGS YOU WILL NEED
Backpack
Several large rocks
Permanent marker

EXPERIMENT
Prior to the experiment, use a permanent marker to label each rock with a different burden that might be faced in life. Place the rocks into the pack, and invite one volunteer to come forward and carry the pack. The load will be extremely heavy. Take the rocks from the pack one at a time and distribute them to other students. The load will then be easier to bear.

GOSPEL APPLICATION
Place the rocks into the pack one at a time as you discuss with the class each burden. When the pack is full, ask for a volunteer to come forward to carry the pack. Invite someone to read aloud Mosiah 18:8. Alma taught that if we want to be called the people of God, we need to be "willing to bear one another's burdens, that they may be light." Remove the rocks from the pack one at a time and hand them to other members of the class. When the load is shared, the burden is much lighter and easier to bear.

ADDITIONAL APPLICATIONS
Freedom through Repentance—Using a permanent marker, label each rock with a different sin. (This can be done prior to your presentation or during class if you want the class

members' input.) Invite one student to come forward, and place the pack on their back. Place the rocks into the pack one at a time. Each sin (rock) makes the pack a little heavier. Soon the pack of "sins" is extremely heavy. Sin weighs us down, depresses us, and makes it hard for us to function mentally and spiritually. When we properly repent of our sins, we can once again enjoy the freedom of righteous living. (Refer to Alma 36:5–24 for a wonderful account of Alma's conversion and remission of sins.)

Shun the Adversary—Satan likes to bring our spirits down by making us believe things about ourselves that just aren't true. We learn in D&C 50:2–3 that Satan and his followers are in this world to deceive and overthrow us. Any negative thought that comes into our mind is from Satan. In Alma 5:40 we learn that "whatsoever is good cometh from God, and whatsoever is evil cometh from the devil." Ask the class to list things that Satan tries to make us believe, and write each of them on a rock. Some examples might be "I'm discouraged," or "I'm worthless." Place the rocks into the pack and ask for a volunteer to come forward to carry the pack. Just as the volunteer is weighed down by the pack of rocks, our spirits are weighed down when we listen to Satan. Through continual prayer we can conquer Satan and his followers (see D&C 10:5). Remove the rocks from the pack so that the volunteer can feel the freedom that comes from shunning the adversary.

BEAR UP YOUR BURDENS

"Beareth all things, believeth all things, hopeth all things, endureth all things." 1 Corinthians 13:7

THINGS YOU WILL NEED
Balloon
Drinking straw
Tape
Heavy book

EXPERIMENT
Stretch the balloon prior to the experiment. Insert the straw into the neck of the balloon and secure tightly with tape. Place the balloon under the book. Blow air through the straw into the balloon, causing the book to be lifted up.

GOSPEL APPLICATION
"My people must be tried in all things," the Lord declared, "that they may be prepared to receive the glory that I have for them, even the glory of Zion; and he that will not bear chastisement is not worthy of my kingdom" (D&C 136:31). In Abraham 3:25–26, we learn that the main reason for our mortal probation is to be tested and tried with hardships and temptations. We cannot escape the trials that exist for our learning. When we are called upon to endure a trial, we should pray that Heavenly Father will strengthen us—that we may be lifted up and our shoulders be made strong enough to carry the weight of the trial. This is demonstrated when the air is blown through the straw and into the balloon, strengthening it and helping it to lift the heavy burden of the book.

BEWARE OF PRIDE

"See that ye are not lifted up unto pride." Alma 38:11

THINGS YOU WILL NEED
Two balloons
A straight pin

EXPERIMENT
Blow up one balloon and, at the appropriate time, pop it with a pin. Blow up the next balloon and, at the appropriate time, let the air out slowly.

GOSPEL APPLICATION
The Book of Mormon is full of warnings about the danger of being puffed up in pride. Pride was always the underlying cause for destruction among the Nephites. Blow air into the first balloon a little at a time as you discuss the prideful ways of the world. Members of the Church are not immune to pride. Discuss some ways we as members of the Church demonstrate pride. When the balloon becomes quite large, tie it off and invite a member of the class to hold it while you continue the demonstration. Blow up the second balloon as you continue to discuss pride. When the second balloon becomes large, invite a class member to hold it, but don't tie it off. Explain to the class that the Lord wants His people to be humble. He can accomplish this in two ways. In D&C 19:20, He warns the unrepentant, "lest I humble you with my almighty power." Having the Lord humble us can be hard, and we deny ourselves valuable blessings. Demonstrate this by popping the balloon that has been tied off. On the other hand, if we choose to repent and humble ourselves, we are truly blessed. Alma 32:16 says, "Therefore, blessed are they who humble themselves without

being compelled to be humble." Demonstrate this by slowly letting the air out of the second balloon. In the end, the balloons are both "without pride," but the first balloon was destroyed in the process, while the second balloon was left intact.

BOUND BY SIN

"Lay aside every sin, which easily doth beset you, which doth bind you down to destruction." Alma 7:15

THINGS YOU WILL NEED
Large laundry bag with drawstring

EXPERIMENT
Ask a class member to step inside the laundry bag. As the presentation progresses, ask the class member to "sink" into the laundry bag as you drawstring it closed around their neck.

GOSPEL APPLICATION
We can learn from the scriptures that sin binds us down unto destruction (see Alma 7:15). We also learn that the devil leads us "with a flaxen cord" until he can bind us "with his strong cords forever" (2 Nephi 26:22). If we keep ourselves free from sin, then we are able to perform the will of God more easily. Demonstrate this by allowing the person to step into the bag without pulling it up yet. The person is still able to read scriptures, take the sacrament, serve others, etc. But as sin sneaks in and we are slowly led away with "flaxen cords," it is much harder to perform the will of God. Demonstrate this by pulling the laundry bag up to the neck of the person and pulling snugly on the drawstring. The person would now have a difficult time reading scriptures, partaking of the sacrament, or serving others. We need to keep ourselves free from sin to avoid the binding power of the devil.

CHASTITY

"Keep thyself unspotted from the world." D&C 59:9

THINGS YOU WILL NEED
    Clear drinking glass with water
    Clay
    Spoon

EXPERIMENT
    Place the glass of water on a table and tap it lightly with the spoon. It should ring out with a clear sound. During the presentation, place small amounts of clay on the outside of the glass. Tap lightly on the glass after each addition of clay. The ringing sound becomes less and less clear until it is just a "clank."

GOSPEL APPLICATION
    Paul counsels in 1 Timothy 4:12, "Let no man despise thy youth; but be thou an example of the believers, in word, in conversation, in charity, in spirit, in faith, in purity." If we want to be an example of purity, we need to "keep [ourselves] unspotted from the world" (James 1:27). In the demonstration, the clear glass of water represents purity—ringing clear and true. When the clay, which represents sin or transgression, is attached to the glass, the sound is altered in a negative way. Sin can alter our lives in a negative way also. By removing the clay from the glass, we can enjoy the beautiful sound once again. Through sincere repentance, we can once again enjoy a life of purity.

CLEANSED THROUGH REPENTANCE

"Let us cleanse ourselves from all filthiness of the flesh and spirit, perfecting holiness in the fear of God." 2 Corinthians 7:1

THINGS YOU WILL NEED
Saucer
Plastic spoon
Salt & pepper
Wool cloth

EXPERIMENT

Pour some salt and a little bit of pepper into the saucer. Mix them together with your finger. First place the plastic spoon over the salt and pepper—close to it but not touching. Nothing should happen. Next, rub the plastic spoon with the wool cloth. Hold the spoon over the salt and pepper again. This time the pepper should stick to the spoon.

Note: If all the pepper does not leave the salt, shake the pepper that has collected on the spoon into another container and start over by rubbing the spoon again.

GOSPEL APPLICATION

Through the Atonement of Jesus Christ, we can be forgiven of our sins. To be truly forgiven takes effort on our part. Demonstrate this by having the pepper represent sin. When nothing is done to the spoon, the pepper (sin) remains. When effort is made by correctly following the repentance process (namely recognition of sin, remorse, confession, restitution, and the commitment to forsake the sin), we can be cleansed and made pure again. Demonstrate this by rubbing the spoon on the woolen cloth and holding the spoon just over the salt and pepper mixture.

CUTTING REMARKS

"If any man offend not in word, the same is a perfect man, and able also to bridle the whole body." James 3:2

THINGS YOU WILL NEED
A potato
A plastic drinking straw

EXPERIMENT
Soak the potato in water for about thirty minutes prior to the lesson. Applying normal pressure, try pushing the straw through the potato. The straw will most likely bend or buckle before penetrating the skin of the potato. Then, with one fast, strong push, thrust the straw straight down through the potato. It should penetrate easily, even coming out the opposite side of the potato.

GOSPEL APPLICATION
In an ideal conversation, our words should be kind and gentle. Demonstrate this by trying gently to push the straw through the potato. In contrast, when we become angry or upset, our words can change and become sharp and cutting. Without thinking, we can use words that can cut straight to a person's heart and offend them. We are reminded in James 3:8 that the untamed tongue can be "full of deadly poison." We should strive to be careful with our words, choosing ones that will uplift and edify.

DECEPTIONS OF THE ADVERSARY

"And thus the devil cheateth their souls, and leadeth them away."
2 Nephi 28:21

THINGS YOU WILL NEED
Small-mouthed bottle
Water
Drinking straw
Plastic tape (like electrician's tape)

EXPERIMENT
Fill the bottle mostly full with water and insert the straw. Place a few pieces of tape tightly around the mouth of the bottle so it forms an airtight seal around the straw. Invite a volunteer to try to suck some water out of the bottle. Make sure they don't take their mouth away from the straw once they begin to drink from it. They should only be able to get a tiny bit of water, if they get anything at all.

GOSPEL APPLICATION
Jesus taught that "whosoever drinketh of the water that I shall give him shall never thirst; but the water that I shall give him shall be in him a well of water springing up into everlasting life" (John 4:14). The bottle filled with water represents the living water of the gospel. In order to partake of the living water that Jesus spoke of, we must live our lives according to His commandments. The adversary, through his lies and deceptions, tries to prevent us from partaking of the living water. If we choose to listen to him, then we are unable to enjoy the full benefits of the gospel. Discuss as a class some of the possible deceptions while you wrap the pieces of tape around the bottle opening, creating an airtight seal. Invite a volunteer to come

forward and try to drink the water. When the volunteer is unsuccessful, remove the pieces of tape. If you wish, discuss ways of avoiding the deceptions of the adversary as you do so. Then invite the volunteer to try to drink again.

DEGREES OF GLORY

"There is one glory of the sun, and another glory of the moon, and another glory of the stars." 1 Corinthians 15:41

THINGS YOU WILL NEED
Various ingredients (see experiment below)
Cracker
Biscuit
Cake with white frosting

EXPERIMENT
Display the cracker, biscuit, and cake on a table. Display the various ingredients it would take to make each item.

GOSPEL APPLICATION
Speaking of the Bible, Joseph Smith wrote, "It appeared self-evident from what truths were left, that if God rewarded every one according to the deeds done in the body, the term 'Heaven,' as intended for the Saints' eternal home, must include more kingdoms than one" (D&C 76, section heading). Later he received a glorious vision of the three degrees of glory. As Paul stated in 1 Corinthians 15:41, "There is one glory of the sun, and another glory of the moon, and another glory of the stars: for one star differeth from another star in glory." Compare this to the different "glory" of the baked items and their corresponding ingredients. With only a few ingredients available, we can only hope to make a cracker. A few more ingredients will yield a biscuit or something similar. But with all the ingredients, we can make a grand and glorious cake with frosting (besides a multitude of other things.) Each kingdom allows us to accomplish certain things. The two lower kingdoms have their limits. We cannot hope to make a "grand and glorious cake" with what

is available in those kingdoms. Only the celestial kingdom will stock the ingredients needed to accomplish such great things.

DISCERNMENT

"I will impart unto you of my Spirit, which shall enlighten your mind, which shall fill your soul with joy." D&C 11:13

THINGS YOU WILL NEED
Scripture references written on strips of paper
A dark room

EXPERIMENT
Prepare the room ahead of time by closing all curtains and doing whatever else is necessary to make the room completely dark when the lights are turned off. Prepare and pass out to class members the following scripture references: D&C 88:67, Micah 7:8, 1 Peter 2:9, 1 John 1:5, Psalm 18:28. Before allowing class members to read their scriptures, turn off the lights in the room—making it difficult or impossible to read. At the appropriate time, turn on the lights and have the class members successfully read their scriptures.

GOSPEL APPLICATION
The darkness of the room makes it difficult, if not impossible, for the class members to read (or discern) their scriptures. Just as the lights in the room help the class members see what to read, the light of the gospel helps us to see how to live our lives.

DISCOMFORT OF SIN

"Let your sins trouble you, with that trouble which shall bring you down unto repentance." Alma 42:29

THINGS YOU WILL NEED
Small pebble or bean for each student

EXPERIMENT
At the beginning of class, give each class member a pebble or bean to place in their shoe. Have them keep it there throughout the lesson.

GOSPEL APPLICATION
Alma counseled his son Corianton to "let your sins trouble you, with that trouble which shall bring you down unto repentance" (Alma 42:29). Just as the pebble causes physical discomfort, sin causes spiritual discomfort through the promptings of the Holy Ghost. To receive physical relief, we can take the pebble out of the shoe. The only relief from sin, on the other hand, is true repentance.

DOUBT NOT

"And all things, whatsoever ye shall ask in prayer, believing, ye shall receive." Matthew 21:22

THINGS YOU WILL NEED
Large pitcher of water
Two clear bowls
Cup
Masking tape

EXPERIMENT
Place a piece of tape near the top of one of the bowls. This will mark where the water level is to be. Ask one volunteer to come forward and slowly pour water into the bowl until the water reaches the mark. Before the first volunteer finishes, ask another volunteer to come forward and use the cup to scoop water out of the bowl as it is being filled. (The water from the cup can be emptied into the extra bowl.) Continue this process until all the water has been poured from the pitcher.

GOSPEL APPLICATION
When teaching His disciples, Jesus said, "For verily I say unto you, That whosoever shall say unto this mountain, Be thou removed, and be thou cast into the sea; and shall not doubt in his heart, but shall believe that those things which he saith shall come to pass; he shall have whatsoever he saith. Therefore I say unto you, What things soever ye desire, when ye pray, believe that ye receive them, and ye shall have them" (Mark 11:23–24). In the demonstration, the water being poured into the bowl represents faith. The person is trying to fill the bowl to the mark. The water being taken from the bowl represents doubt. As long as we have doubt, we will never

accomplish our desires. James 1:6 states, "But let him ask in faith, nothing wavering." If you wish, ask the first volunteer to perform the experiment again without doubt to show the successfulness of sufficient faith.

ENDURE TO THE END

"He that is faithful and endureth shall overcome the world."
D&C 63:47

THINGS YOU WILL NEED
A sprouting potato
Pot filled with moist soil
Shoe box
Scrap cardboard
Tape

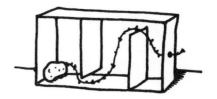

EXPERIMENT
A few days before you plan to use this experiment, complete the following preparations. Plant the potato in the moist soil. Place the shoe box on its side and place the pot in the corner of the shoe box. Cut a hole in the shoe box at the opposite end. Cut scraps of cardboard and tape them in place as shown in the diagram above to create a maze. (Be sure to leave the appropriate gaps at the top or bottom of the cardboard scraps so the plant can grow through the maze.) Place the lid securely on the shoe box and place it in a window. After a few days, the shoot will have made its way to the light.

GOSPEL APPLICATION
We are promised eternal life if we "press forward, feasting upon the word of Christ, and endure to the end" (2 Nephi 31:20). Carefully remove the lid from the shoe box and show how the sprout was determined to grow toward the light. By doing so, it was able to overcome the obstacles that were placed in its way. Through determination and commitment, we can overcome obstacles, endure to the end, and enjoy the blessings of eternal life.

ADDITIONAL APPLICATIONS

Overcoming Obstacles—We can more easily overcome any obstacle placed before us by focusing on the Light.

Diligence—"All victory and glory is brought to pass unto you through your diligence, faithfulnesss, and prayers of faith" (D&C 103:36).

ENTANGLE NOT IN SIN

"Entangle not yourselves in sin, but let your hands be clean, until the Lord comes." D&C 88:86

THINGS YOU WILL NEED
Rope or twine

EXPERIMENT
After showing the unknotted rope to the class, tie the rope into several knots—some tight, some loose. When the time is appropriate during the lesson, try to untie the knots.

GOSPEL APPLICATION
Hold the rope for the class to see. This represents someone who is virtually free from sin. As a mistake is made, though, it's like tying a knot in our otherwise clean, untangled life. Some sins are more serious than others, just as some knots are tighter than others. In D&C 88:86, we are counseled to "entangle not ourselves in sin, but let our hands be clean, until the Lord comes." With some effort on our part, we can be forgiven of our sins through the Atonement of Jesus Christ. Some sins take more time and effort to repent of, just like the tighter knots take more time and effort to untie compared to the loose knots. We should all strive to keep our lives untangled and free from sin.

ADDITIONAL APPLICATION
Testimony—Testimonies are like knots in a rope. Some testimonies have been made strong by trials and tribulations—just as some knots are made strong by pulling and tugging at the ends of the rope to tighten and strengthen the knot. Some testimonies have not been tested and are weaker—just as some knots are loose from lack of opposition at each end of the rope.

Just as it is harder to undo a tight knot compared to a loose knot, it is harder to "undo" a strong testimony compared to a weak one. If we were hanging by a rope over the edge of a cliff, we would want to be sure that the knots anchoring the rope to solid ground were strong enough to keep us from falling. We should have the same desire to make sure our testimony is strong enough to keep us from falling into the hands of the adversary.

ETERNAL BLISS

"Give heed to the word of Christ, which will point to you a straight course to eternal bliss." Alma 37:44

THINGS YOU WILL NEED
Two mirrors (one hand-held, one larger)

EXPERIMENT
Hold the hand mirror to your face (facing away from you) as you stand in front of the larger mirror. When adjusted correctly, you will see the reflection continuing without end.

GOSPEL APPLICATION
Alma counseled his son Helaman to "give heed to the word of Christ, which will point to you a straight course to eternal bliss" (Alma 37:44). To get an idea of eternity, have the class members take turns holding the hand mirror in front of the larger mirror. If we follow the words of Christ, we will enjoy eternal life.

EVEN BALANCE

"Let me be weighed in an even balance, that God may know mine integrity." Job 31:6

THINGS YOU WILL NEED
    Hammer
    10" piece of string
    12" ruler

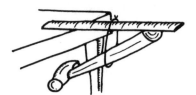

EXPERIMENT
    Tie the ends of the string together, forming a simple loop. Place the loop around the ruler and the handle of the hammer. Suspend the ruler from the edge of the table as shown in the illustration above. Adjust the string so that the hammer and ruler are balanced and suspended from the edge of the table.
    Note: Be careful when adjusting the string so that the hammer doesn't fall on your toes!

GOSPEL APPLICATION
    Sometimes we get caught up in the desire to attain riches, secular knowledge, or pleasure. If these are our only desires, we will become unbalanced and be stopped in our progression toward eternal salvation. In D&C 11:23, the Lord counseled Hyrum Smith to "seek the kingdom of God, and all things shall be added according to that which is just." We should follow the same counsel and put the gospel at the center of our lives. By doing so, we will have the proper balance and continue to progress toward exaltation. To demonstrate this, let the hammer and ruler represent riches and secular knowledge. When each item is suspended from the edge of the table by itself, it falls. The gospel is represented by the string. Place the string around the ruler and the handle of the hammer and suspend the ruler

from the edge of a table. Adjust the string so that everything is balanced and suspended freely. (Refer to the illustration.) As Jacob taught the Nephites, "But before ye seek for riches, seek ye for the kingdom of God. And after ye have obtained a hope in Christ ye shall obtain riches, if ye seek them; and ye will seek them for the intent to do good" (Jacob 2:18–19). If we put Christ at the center of our lives, He will bless us with our other righteous desires.

ADDITIONAL APPLICATION

Self-mastery—In Alma 38:12, Alma counseled his son Shiblon to "bridle all your passions." We also learn from Proverbs 25:28, "He that hath no rule over his own spirit is like a city that is broken down, and without walls." We cannot find true happiness when we are servants to uncontrollable passions and appetites. Our spirits are more powerful than our bodies, and Heavenly Father has promised us that we will not be "tempted above that ye are able" and that he will also "make a way to escape" (1 Corinthians 10:13). By gaining control over our passions, we will attain a balance in our lives that will help us reach exaltation. Demonstrate this by placing the loop of string around the ruler and the handle of the hammer. The ruler and the hammer represent worldly passions and appetites. The string represents self-mastery. Place the ruler at the edge of the table. When adjusted properly, the string prevents the ruler and hammer from becoming unbalanced and falling to the ground.

EXAMPLES

"Be thou an example of the believers, in word, in conversation, in charity, in spirit, in faith, in purity." 1 Timothy 4:12

THINGS YOU WILL NEED
Leaves
Crayon
Paper

EXPERIMENT
Place the paper on top of the leaf and rub over the leaf with the side of a crayon. The image of the leaf will transfer to the paper.

GOSPEL APPLICATION
Just as Christ was an example to us, we need to be an example to others. 1 Timothy 4:12 states, "Let no man despise thy youth; but be thou an example of the believers, in word, in conversation, in charity, in spirit, in faith, in purity." Our good example can "rub off" on others and influence them to do good also. Demonstrate this by doing a rubbing of the leaf. Show how the leaf and the rubbing are alike. We must be watchful, however, because a bad example can rub off also. Demonstrate this by tearing away a part of another leaf (representing sin). Do a rubbing of the partial leaf. Compare the two rubbings. Each rubbing duplicates the image of the leaf that was used. We must always strive to set good examples to those around us.

ADDITIONAL APPLICATION
Created in God's Image—We learn in Genesis 1:26 and in Moses 6:9 that we were created in the image of God. Demonstrate what it means to be in created the image of something by doing

several rubbings of various items such as leaves, flat lace, or embossed images. When we compare the two, we can see the image of the original in each rubbing.

FAITH

"If ye will have faith in me ye shall have power to do whatsoever thing is expedient in me." Moroni 7:33

THINGS YOU WILL NEED
Clear goblet (or similar glass)
Dried peas
Dinner plate
Water

EXPERIMENT
Fill the goblet to overflowing with peas. Carefully pour water up to the brim of the goblet and set it on the dinner plate. In a short while, the peas will swell and overflow onto the plate.

GOSPEL APPLICATION
The dried peas in the goblet represent the many blessings that Heavenly Father has in store for us. We need to apply faith in order to "activate" the blessings. Moroni 10:7 states, "Wherefore I would exhort you that ye deny not the power of God; for he worketh by power, according to the faith of the children of men." Without faith on our part, Heavenly Father is limited in how much He can bless us. When we exercise faith, the blessings will swell and overflow in our lives.

ADDITIONAL APPLICATION
Missionary Efforts—When we share the gospel with our nonmember friends and relatives, their hearts can begin to swell and overflow with the Spirit.

FAULT FINDING

"Cease to find fault one with another." D&C 88:124

THINGS YOU WILL NEED
  Empty narrow-necked bottle
  Small wad of paper

EXPERIMENT
  Hold the bottle horizontal and place the small wad of paper just inside the neck. Try to blow the paper into the bottle with a sharp burst of air. Instead of going into the bottle, the wad of paper will fly back towards your face.

GOSPEL APPLICATION
  Matthew 15:11 states, "Not that which goeth into the mouth defileth a man; but that which cometh out of the mouth, this defileth a man." We also learn in Matthew 7:1–2, "Judge not, that ye be not judged. For with what judgment ye judge, ye shall be judged: and with what measure ye mete, it shall be measured to you again." The small wad of paper represents our judgment of others. When we judge others (represented by blowing into the bottle) that judgment comes back to us and is used to measure us also. Matthew 7:5 reminds us to "first cast out the beam out of thine own eye; and then shalt thou see clearly to cast out the mote out of thy brother's eye."

ADDITIONAL APPLICATION
  Unkind Words—We are advised to "keep thy tongue from evil, and thy lips from speaking guile" (Psalm 34:13). This advice not only protects others, but protects ourselves. When we use unkind words, often they return to us in undesirable ways. Demonstrate this by writing the unkind words on the slip

of paper and performing the experiment as directed. Another good piece of advice can be found in Proverbs 21:23: "Whoso keepeth his mouth and his tongue keepeth his soul from troubles."

FELLOWSHIPPING

"And this commandment have we from him, that he who loveth
God love his brother also." 1 John 4:21

THINGS YOU WILL NEED
Balloon
Measuring tape
Access to a refrigerator

EXPERIMENT
Completely fill the ballon with air and tie it securely.
Measure and note the circumference of the balloon. Place the
ballon in a refrigerator for thirty minutes. Upon removal,
measure and take note of the circumference again. The balloon
should have shrunk in size.

GOSPEL APPLICATION
Moroni taught that after new converts are baptized and
have received the Holy Ghost, they are then numbered among
the people of the Church, and their names are taken "that they
might be remembered and nourished by the good word of God,
to keep them in the right way, to keep them continually
watchful unto prayer" (Moroni 6:4). As members of Christ's
church, we have a duty to remember and nourish these new
converts. If we fail to fellowship with sincere warmth and love,
the testimony of the new members could become cold and will
shrink.

ADDITIONAL APPLICATION
Spiritual Warmth—Our spirits need continual warmth
from the gospel. If they are left uncared for and become spiritually cold, they will shrink.

FIRM FOUNDATION

"Nevertheless the foundation of God standeth sure."
2 Timothy 2:19

THINGS YOU WILL NEED
2 or 3 large books (such as dictionaries or encyclopedias)
Several sheets of newspaper
A hammer
A thick wooden board (preferably a 2x4)
Nails

EXPERIMENT
While sitting, stack the books on your lap. Place a thick layer of newspaper on top of the books to protect them. Place the board on top of the newspaper. Now pound a nail into the board while holding it in your lap. At the appropriate time in the lesson, place the stack on the floor and pound another nail into the board. You could even have a volunteer carefully pound the nails if you wished. You will find that it is much easier to pound the nail into the board when it is on a solid surface.

GOSPEL APPLICATION
In Matthew 7:24–27, Jesus teaches us the wisdom of building a house on a firm foundation. When we build our lives on the gospel of Jesus Christ, we are better able to withstand the trials that may come to us. Our faith can lighten our burdens and give us strength to accomplish great things. Demonstrate the power of a firm foundation by first trying to pound the nail into the wood while it is on your lap. It will be quite difficult. Then demonstrate how much easier it is to do the same task when the board is placed on a firm foundation. The firm foundation gives more support and makes the job easier.

GOSSIPING

"Whoso keepeth his mouth and his tongue keepeth his soul from troubles." Proverbs 21:23

THINGS YOU WILL NEED

Blotting paper (found at art supply stores), cut into four narrow strips
Four different black ink pens
Shallow bowl or saucer
Water

EXPERIMENT

Prior to the lesson, place one large dot of ink 1" from one end of each strip of blotting paper. Use a different marker for each strip. Place the dotted end of each strip into the saucer of water. Let them sit as the water separates the ink in each dot.

GOSPEL APPLICATION

We are commanded in Leviticus 19:16 not to be tale-bearers—or in other words, not to gossip. Spreading gossip is harmful because facts are lost when stories are retold—giving an unfair perception of the one who is the subject of the gossip. Proverbs 18:8 says, "The words of a talebearer are as wounds, and they go down into the innermost parts of the belly." Proverbs 21:23 offers good advice: "Whoso keepeth his mouth and his tongue keepeth his soul from troubles." In the demonstration, the black dots represent the same story being told to four different people. All four people hear the same story to begin with, but as they retell their versions, some things might be added and some things might be omitted. This is demonstrated by the various ways the inks are separated by the water.

ADDITIONAL APPLICATION

Talents—In D&C 46:11 we learn that each of us is given different gifts (or talents) by the Spirit of God. We also learn in Moroni 10:18, 30 that these gifts come from Christ and that we should "lay hold upon every good gift." To demonstrate that each of us is individual and has been given different gifts, place the four strips in the saucer of water. As the ink separates, it represents the various gifts that are within each of us. Each dot of ink separates differently, just as each one of us possesses different talents. Some of us may not even realize the different talents that lie within us until we truly search for, find, and exercise them.

HELPING OTHERS

"When ye are in the service of your fellow beings ye are only in the service of your God." Mosiah 2:17

THINGS YOU WILL NEED
Modeling clay (not Play-doh)
Clear glass bowl filled with water

EXPERIMENT
Begin by shaping four balls, three small and one large, from the clay. Drop the balls of clay into the bowl of water. Each one sinks to the bottom. Remove the largest ball of clay and shape it into a boat. Float it on top of the water. Retrieve the other balls and place them in the boat. The boat supports itself and the other clay balls.

GOSPEL APPLICATION
In Mosiah 18:8–9 we learn that part of our commitment at baptism is to be willing to "bear one another's burdens," "mourn with those that mourn," and "comfort those that stand in need of comfort." The three small balls of clay represent three different people—one who is laden with burdens, one who is mourning, and one who is in need of comfort. Explain this to your class as you drop each ball into the water. Roll the larger ball of clay in your hands as you explain that if we are all "rolled up" in ourselves, we will not be able to help those in need. Demonstrate this by dropping the larger ball of clay into the water also. Each ball sinks. Remove the larger ball of clay from the water. Stretch and shape the clay into a small "boat"— symbolic of the stretching and shaping we need to do in our own lives in order to help others. We need to be flexible and giving and willing to help those around us. Float the clay boat

on the water. Retrieve the smaller balls and place them in the boat to show how we can help support others in their times of need.

ADDITIONAL APPLICATION

Strengthen Thy Brethren—Luke 22:32 states, ". . . and when thou art converted, strengthen thy brethren." The small balls of clay could represent nonmembers, new members, or less-active members who are not totally converted to the gospel of Jesus Christ. When dropped into the water, they sink. (Do not place the larger ball into the water.) The larger ball of clay represents someone who has been converted to the gospel of Jesus Christ. Read Luke 22:32 as you shape the clay into a small boat. Float the boat on the water. Place the balls of clay into the boat. This demonstrates that by "spreading" the gospel we can support and strengthen others who are not yet converted to the gospel of Jesus Christ.

HIDDEN SINS

"Ye cannot hide your crimes from God; and except ye repent they will stand as a testimony against you at the last day." Alma 39:8

THINGS YOU WILL NEED
    Two tablets of any laxative (not chocolate flavored) containing phenolphthalein
    One tablespoon rubbing alcohol
    Wet bar of white soap
    Tub of water
    Hand towel

EXPERIMENT
    Crush the two tablets into a fine powder and add the rubbing alcohol to form a paste. Rub the paste onto a volunteer's hands and let dry. Give the volunteer a wet bar of white soap. The chemical reaction of the laxative and soap should cause the volunteer's hands to turn a fuchsia color.

GOSPEL APPLICATION
    We may be able to hide our transgressions from those around us, but we can never hide our sins from Heavenly Father. Alma 39:8 states, "But behold, ye cannot hide your crimes from God; and except ye repent they will stand as a testimony against you at the last day." When we reach the end of our mortal existence, we will stand before God to be judged of Him. If we are not clean, our sins will be "as scarlet," not "white as snow" (Isaiah 1:18). The dried paste represents our hidden sins. Our sins may not be completely noticeable to those around us, but when we stand in front of the Lord to be judged (the wet bar of soap), our sins will be made known.

Note: The paste could be placed on the hand of the teacher ahead of time so that the class is completely unaware of the "sins" until they are made known by the wet bar of soap.

ADDITIONAL APPLICATION

Cleansed through the Blood of Christ—We learn in Mosiah 4:2 that the people in King Benjamin's time cried unto the Lord for mercy. They desired forgiveness of their sins, and this was only possible through the atoning blood of Jesus Christ. Revelation 1:5 states, "And from Jesus Christ, who is the faithful witness, and the first begotten of the dead, and the prince of the kings of the earth. Unto him that loved us, and washed us from our sins in his own blood." It is only through the blood of Christ that we can be washed from our sins. The dried paste represents sin. As the hands are washed with the soap, the "atoning blood" is revealed. Continue to wash with the soap until the hands are completely clean.

HIDDEN TREASURES

"And all saints who . . . keep and do these sayings . . . shall find . . . great treasures of knowledge, even hidden treasures." D&C 89:18–19

THINGS YOU WILL NEED
Several coins
Large opaque bowl
"Fun-Tack" or clear tape
Pitcher of water

EXPERIMENT
Prior to the lesson, secure the coins to the inside bottom of the bowl with "Fun-Tack" or clear tape. During the lesson invite a volunteer to come forward and look over the edge of the bowl at the coins. Then ask the volunteer to move backward until they can no longer see the coins at the bottom of the bowl and then stop. During the demonstration, slowly pour the water into the bowl a little at a time until the volunteer can see the coins again from where they are standing.

Note: This optical illusion occurs when the bowl is full of water and the light bends so that your volunteer is able to see the reflection of the coins.

GOSPEL APPLICATION
In D&C 89:18–19 we find a wonderful promise given by the Lord to all obedient Saints. Those who keep the Word of Wisdom "shall find wisdom and great treasures of knowledge, even hidden treasures." After your volunteer has moved backward and is in a position where they can no longer see the coins, discuss the various "words of wisdom" given in section 89. With each principle discussed, pour a little bit of the water

into the bowl—symbolizing obedience to the principle. Eventually, when the bowl is full of water, the volunteer's "obedience" will bring into view the great treasures of knowledge and wisdom (symbolized by the coins) that were once hidden from sight.

THE HOLY GHOST–1

"And by the power of the Holy Ghost ye may know the truth of all things." Moroni 10:5

THINGS YOU WILL NEED

Two paper cups
A 6'–8' piece of string
Two paper clips
5 blank envelopes

EXPERIMENT

Carefully poke a small hole in the bottom of each of the two cups. Thread one end of the string through the bottom of one cup and tie the string to a paper clip. (The paper clip will be on the inside of the cup.) Thread the other end of the string through the bottom of the other cup and tie it to a paper clip in the same fashion. Set aside. Label each envelope with a word or phrase that describes something that would interfere with hearing the Holy Ghost, such as selfishness, sin, pride, and preoccupation with wordly things. At the appropriate time during the demonstration, pull the string taut and hang the envelopes from it.

GOSPEL APPLICATION

We learn in D&C 85:6 that the Holy Ghost is "the still small voice, which whispereth through and pierceth all things." Through him we receive truth, comfort, and revelation from Heavenly Father. His voice can be as a whisper, and we need to be spiritually in tune to hear him. Demonstrate this by having a volunteer hold one of the cups to their ear, and as you pull the string taut, speak softly into the other cup. Your voice will be carried along the string and will be heard by the volunteer.

Point out that the string is free from interference and therefore can carry the message without interruption. Sometimes we are not in tune to the whisperings of the Spirit. Some of our choices and actions will cause interference. In Helaman 4:24, the Nephites found that their actions were preventing them from hearing the Spirit of the Lord. While the string is tight, have someone hang the flaps of the pre-labeled envelopes over the string. Speak softly again to the person while the envelopes hang on the string. Your voice will be nearly impossible to hear. Discuss how each thing would interfere with your hearing the Holy Ghost and why it is important to keep the line of communication open and free of interference.

ADDITIONAL APPLICATION

Prayer—Proverbs 15:29 says, "The Lord is far from the wicked: but he heareth the prayer of the righteous." When we keep the lines of communication open between us and the Lord by righteous living, it is easier for our prayers to be heard and answered. Unrighteous acts cause interference and make it difficult to communicate with the Lord.

THE HOLY GHOST—2

"Quench not the Spirit." 1 Thessalonians 5:19

THINGS YOU WILL NEED
Small styrofoam container with lid
Alarm clock
Four washcloths

EXPERIMENT
This presentation progresses in different steps. The first step is to sound the alarm clock. Next, sound the alarm and place it in the styrofoam container, then close the lid. The third step is to place four washcloths at the bottom of the container, sound the alarm and place it on top of the washcloth, then close the lid. With each step, the sound gets more muffled.

GOSPEL APPLICATION
All of us who have repented, been baptized, and received the gift of the Holy Ghost are entitled to receive the Spirit's promptings. We can continue to enjoy the promptings of the Holy Ghost as long as we remain worthy. This is represented by sounding the alarm. John 8:47 states, "He that is of God heareth God's words: ye therefore hear them not, because ye are not of God." When we choose to sin, we are not of God and therefore muffle the promptings of the Holy Ghost, as demonstrated in the second and third steps of the presentation. The Lord warns in Mosiah 26:28, "Therefore I say unto you, that he that will not hear my voice, the same shall ye not receive into my church, for him I will not receive at the last day.

ADDITIONAL APPLICATIONS
Muffled Cries to the Lord—Speaking to the unrepentant, the Lord warns in Mosiah 11:24, "Yea, and it shall come to pass

that when they shall cry unto me I will be slow to hear their cries; yea, and I will suffer them that they be smitten by their enemies." We also learn in John 9:31, "Now we know that God heareth not sinners: but if any man be a worshipper of God, and doeth his will, him he heareth." Do we muffle our cries to the Lord through unrepentant acts?

The Needs of Others—Do we hear the needs of others, or do we cover up their cries with other things in our lives? The washcloths and styrofoam container could represent various selfish desires that muffle the cries of others.

A HOUSE OF GOD

"But as for me and my house, we will serve the Lord."
Joshua 24:15

THINGS YOU WILL NEED

Large, clear glass bowl
Clear jar
Photograph of a family
Pitcher of water
Food coloring

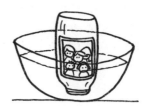

EXPERIMENT

Place the photograph upside down in the jar. Be sure it fits snugly (use tape if needed) so that it doesn't fall out when the jar is turned over. Fill the bowl about halfway with water. At the appropriate time, place several drops of food coloring into the water. Turn the jar upside down and place it straight down into the bowl of water. The air should be trapped inside the jar, protecting the family picture from the water.

GOSPEL APPLICATION

Put several drops of food coloring in the bowl of water as you talk about how the world around us continues to grow more wicked every day. To combat this, we need to do all we can to make our homes a place of refuge from the evils of the world. D&C 88:119 counsels, "Organize yourselves; prepare every needful thing; and establish a house, even a house of prayer, a house of fasting, a house of faith, a house of learning, a house of gory, a house of order, a house of God." As we follow this counsel, our families will be protected from the wickedness that surrounds us. As we strive to serve the Lord, our homes will be a fortress against evil. Demonstrate this by placing the jar upside down in the bowl of colored water. Remove the jar and show the students how the "home" protected the family from the "wickedness of the world."

HUMILITY

"Be thou humble; and the Lord thy God shall lead thee by the hand, and give thee answer to thy prayers." D&C 112:10

THINGS YOU WILL NEED
Balloon
Wide-mouth jar

EXPERIMENT
This experiment is done in two steps. The first step is to blow air into the balloon. Then, while holding tightly to the neck of the balloon, try to use the filled balloon to lift the jar. The second step is to let the air out of the balloon, then refill the balloon while it is suspended in the mouth of the jar. When the balloon is filled the second time, it will press against the inside of the jar and allow you to lift the jar as you lift the balloon.

GOSPEL APPLICATION
James 4:10 states, "Humble yourselves in the sight of the Lord, and he shall lift you up." In the beginning of the experiment, the filled balloon represents our being puffed up with pride. We are not sufficiently humble to do as the Lord requests. This is represented by trying to lift the jar with the filled balloon. But when we strip ourselves of pride and humble ourselves before the Lord (deflate the balloon), we allow Him to work within us and lift us to the point where we can perform any labors that He requests of us.

ADDITIONAL APPLICATIONS
Strengthen Thy Brethren—In Luke 22:32, Christ said unto Simon, "When thou art converted, strengthen thy brethren." When we receive a testimony of the gospel of Jesus

Christ, we need to use it to help strengthen and lift those around us.

Faith—D&C 8:10 reminds us that "without faith you can do nothing; therefore ask in faith." On the other hand, Mark 9:23 teaches us that "all things are possible to him that believeth." To demonstrate these principles, begin with an uninflated balloon. It is impossible to lift the jar with an uninflated balloon (representing a lack of faith). But when we are filled with faith, we have success. Demonstrate this by filling the balloon with air while it is suspended inside the mouth of the jar.

IN HIS IMAGE

"Let us make man in our image, after our likeness." Genesis 1:26

THINGS YOU WILL NEED
Picture from newspaper
Water
Turpentine
Liquid detergent
Spoon
Sponge
Plain paper
Small bowl

EXPERIMENT
In a bowl, mix two spoonfuls of water, one spoonful of turpentine, and one spoonful of liquid detergent. Using the sponge, dab this mixture onto the newspaper picture. Lay a plain piece of paper over the top of the picture and rub vigorously with the back of a spoon. Carefully peel away the paper to reveal the image of the picture transferred to the plain paper.

GOSPEL APPLICATION
God said in Genesis 1:26, "Let us make man in our image, after our likeness." Use the demonstration to show that an image is a direct resemblance of something else. By looking at our image, we can determine God's image, just as the duplicate picture gives us an idea of what the original picture looks like.

ADDITIONAL APPLICATION
Spreading the Gospel—We can spread the gospel with hard work and diligence (vigorously rubbing with the spoon.)

INTELLIGENCE

"Whatever principle of intelligence we attain unto in this life, it
will rise with us in the resurrection." D&C 130:18

THINGS YOU WILL NEED
Two balloons of equal size—
one filled with helium,
the other filled with air
Permanent marker
Scriptures

EXPERIMENT
Prior to the start of class, use a permanent marker to carefully write the words "knowlegde" and "intelligence" on the
helium-filled balloon. On the air-filled balloon, write words like
"money," "fame," and "worldly possessions." Attach both
balloons to the table, or hold onto each, so that the class does
not realize that the balloons are filled differently. When both
balloons are released at the same time, the helium-filled balloon
will rise, while the air-filled balloon will not.

GOSPEL APPLICATION
In D&C 130:18–19, we learn that the knowledge and intelligence we obtain in this life will rise with us in the resurrection
and benefit us in the world to come. To demonstrate this principle, release both balloons at the same time and watch as the
helium-filled balloon rises and the air-filled balloon does not.

ADDITIONAL APPLICATION
Second Coming of Christ—Prior to the lesson, place a
picture of the Second Coming of Christ high on the classroom
wall. D&C 5:35 states, "And if thou art faithful in keeping my

commandments, thou shalt be lifted up at the last day." Prior to the start of class, use a permanent marker to carefully draw a happy face and the words "faithful in keeping the commandments" on a white, helium-filled balloon. Draw a sad face and the words "unfaithful in keeping the commandments" on a black, air-filled balloon. (This can be done with a white paint pen.) Attach both balloons to the table, or hold onto each, so that the class does not realize the balloons are filled differently. Invite someone to read aloud D&C 5:35 as you release the balloons. The "faithful" balloon will rise up to meet the Savior, and the "unfaithful" balloon fall to the ground.

Note: You could carry this experiment one step further by referring to D&C 29:17 and destroying (popping) the "unfaithful" balloon.

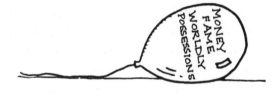

INVISIBLE SINS?

"Cleanse thou me from secret faults." Psalm 19:12

THINGS YOU WILL NEED
Two clear glasses of water
Iodine
Clear lighter fluid

EXPERIMENT
Display the clear glasses of water for the class to see. Place a few drops of iodine in one, and a few drops of lighter fluid in the other. (Note: If iodine and lighter fluid are not available, use red food coloring and water in separate containers labeled "Iodine" and "Lighter Fluid.")

GOSPEL APPLICATION
Begin by explaining to the class that you have before them two different poisons—both equally dangerous. Place each poison in a glass and point out that it's easy to see the poison in the one glass and almost impossible to see the poison in the other. Explain that some transgressions are easy to see, like breaking the Word of Wisdom or swearing. Other sins, like pride, lustful thoughts, and envy, are harder to see but are just as serious. Are we sometimes guilty of judging others by their visible sins when we may have "invisible" sins of our own? We need to be aware of these "invisible" sins and guard against them in our personal lives. (Note: If using actual poisons, be sure to use extra caution so that they are not ingested accidentally!)

LACK OF SPIRITUALITY

"For the Spirit of the Lord will not always strive with man."
2 Nephi 26:11

THINGS YOU WILL NEED
Bowl
Ice cubes
Rice

EXPERIMENT
Place the ice cubes in the bowl. Sprinkle some rice on the table next to the bowl. Invite a volunteer to come forward and place their hand in the bowl of ice for 30 seconds. Have the volunteer dry their hand and then try to pick up some of the grains of rice. Because their sense of touch has been dulled by the coldness, it will be hard to do.

GOSPEL APPLICATION
Nephi warns us in 2 Nephi 26:11 that "the Spirit of the Lord will not always strive with man. And when the Spirit ceaseth to strive with man then cometh speedy destruction." As the volunteer puts their hand into the ice water, discuss some of the reasons the Spirit of God would cease to dwell with man. When we distance ourselves from spiritual things by putting off things such as Church service, scripture study, and prayer, we become "cold" to the enlightenment of the Spirit. For this experiment, the grains of rice represent bits of spiritual enlightenment given to us by the power of the Holy Ghost. When the Spirit is unable to dwell within us because of sin, slothfulness, contention, etc., it becomes difficult to gain spiritual bits of wisdom, knowledge, and understanding. Demonstrate this by having the volunteer try to pick up the

grains of rice with their cold hand. This should be a difficult task. Fortunately, with some work, we can once again enjoy the influence of the Spirit by "warming" ourselves with prayer, scripture study, service to others, etc. Have the volunteer warm their hand by vigorously rubbing both hands together. Now, with a warm hand, they should be successful in picking up "spiritual bits of wisdom and knowledge."

LET YOUR LIGHT SHINE

"Let your light so shine before men, that they may see your good works, and glorify your Father which is in heaven." Matthew 5:16

THINGS YOU WILL NEED
Clear plastic bottle
Pointed scissors
Water
Flashlight
Clear glass bowl

EXPERIMENT
Set the bottle and bowl side by side on a table. With the scissors, carefully poke a hole in the bottle about an inch above the height of the bowl. Place your finger over the hole (or place duct tape over it) and fill the bottle with water. Place the bottle next to the bowl and have someone turn off the lights. Uncover the hole and shine the flashlight through the bottle as the water streams from the bottle and into the bowl. The brightness of the stream of water will vary depending on where you shine the flashlight. When the flashlight is positioned correctly, the water in the bowl should be illuminated also.

GOSPEL APPLICATION
While preaching the Sermon on the Mount, Jesus taught, "Let your light so shine before men, that they may see your good works, and glorify your Father which is in heaven" (Matthew 5:16). Jesus set the perfect example of good works for us to follow. In 3 Nephi 18:16 Christ told the Nephites, "Behold I am the light; I have set an example for you." If we have faith in Him and follow His example, we will be "sure and steadfast, always abounding in good works, being led to glorify God" (Ether

12:4). Just as the light from the flashlight illuminates the stream of water and the water in the bowl, we can illuminate others as we follow the example of Jesus.

LINKING GENERATIONS

"Whatsoever ye shall seal on earth shall be sealed in heaven."
Helaman 10:7

THINGS YOU WILL NEED

 Several 1" strips of paper
 Stapler or tape
 Ink pen
 Scissors

EXPERIMENT

On each strip of paper, write a member of a generation, such as grandparent, parent, child, and grandchild. Make the strips into a paper chain by placing the "generations" in their proper order. Hold the chain for the class to see. At the appropriate time in the presentation, cut one of the links, allowing it—and the others attached to it—to fall to the floor.

GOSPEL APPLICATION

In Helaman 10:7 the Lord said to Nephi, "Behold, I give unto you power, that whatsoever ye shall seal on earth shall be sealed in heaven." Through this same sealing power, we have the opportunity to link many generations of family together. We have a responsibility to other generations to keep our link secure. If one link is broken, it can have devastating effects on all generations. At this point, cut whichever link best fits your class. For example, if you are teaching parents, cut the "parents" link to show how future generations can be cut off. Do we really want to be responsible for breaking the link in our families?

LOST SHEEP

"And if it so be that he find it, verily I say unto you, he rejoiceth more of that sheep, than of the ninety and nine which went not astray." Matthew 18:13

THINGS YOU WILL NEED
Old fluorescent light tube
Plastic wrap
Dark room

EXPERIMENT
In a dark room, rub the fluorescent tube with plastic wrap. The tube will glow where it has been rubbed.

GOSPEL APPLICATION
In Matthew 18:12–14, Jesus taught the parable of the lost sheep. This parable teaches us that all are important to the Lord, especially those who are lost. As members of Christ's church, it is our duty to find His lost sheep. We may find someone who appears to have lost all feeling toward the gospel, but with sincere love and fellowship, we can help them find the glow that is still within.

THE LOVE OF GOD

"The love of God, which sheddeth itself abroad in the hearts of the
children of men . . . is the most desirable above all things."
1 Nephi 11:22

THINGS YOU WILL NEED
White frosting
Plastic spoons

EXPERIMENT
Give each person a spoonful of frosting during the lesson as
you discuss the love of God.

GOSPEL APPLICATION
Lehi's vision of the tree of life helps us to understand the
sweetness and beauty of the gospel. Lehi said, "And it came to pass
that I beheld a tree, whose fruit was desirable to make one happy.
And it came to pass that I did go forth and partake of the fruit
thereof, and I beheld that it was most sweet, above all that I ever
before tasted" (1 Nephi 8:10–11). After Lehi partook of the fruit,
his soul was filled with "exceedingly great joy" and he was desirous
for his family to partake also (1 Nephi 8:12). In 1 Nephi 11:25,
Nephi learned that the tree of life represents the love of God. The
sweet, white frosting represents the fruit that Lehi partook of in
his dream. As you explain that Lehi was desirous to share the fruit
with his family, share the frosting with the members of the class.
Encourage everyone to share the sweetness of the gospel with
others so that they too can enjoy the sweetness of the love of God.

ADDITIONAL APPLICATION
Spreading the Gospel—In this experiment you will also
need small cookies or graham crackers and a knife to spread the

frosting. Pass out the cookies to the class members, but instruct them not to eat them yet. In Mosiah 3:20, King Benjamin foretold a time when the "knowledge of a Savior shall spread throughout every nation, kindred, tongue, and people." In order for this to happen, we need to do our part in spreading the gospel. As a class, discuss various ways of spreading the gospel. Joseph Smith once said, "We don't ask any people to throw away any good they have got; we only ask them to come and get more" (*History of the Church* [Salt Lake City: Deseret Book, 1967], 5:259). The class members already have something good (the cookie). Now share more goodness with them by spreading the frosting, representing the gospel, onto each cookie.

LOVE ONE ANOTHER

"Let us love one another: for love is of God; and every one that
loveth is born of God, and knoweth God." 1 John 4:7

THINGS YOU WILL NEED
Clear drinking glass filled
with one cup of water
One fresh egg
Salt (about 1/4 cup)
Tablespoon
Permanent marker

EXPERIMENT
Prior to the experiment, carefully draw a face on the egg
with a permanent marker (optional). Place the egg in the glass
of water to demonstrate how it sinks to the bottom. Remove
the egg and stir in the salt, one tablespoon at a time. When all
the salt has been added, replace the egg to demonstrate that it
now floats.

GOSPEL APPLICATION
Carefully place the egg in the water and explain that the egg
represents someone who is not receiving love from others. It
sinks to the bottom. In John 15:12, we learn that it is a
commandment to love one another. Remove the egg from the
water and set it aside. Stir the salt into the water one table-
spoonful at a time as you mention various ways to show love for
others. Replace the egg to demonstrate how the egg is now supported with "love" and floats instead of sinks. Note: This experiment could be used to demonstrate the need to show love to
family members, ward members, neighbors, etc.

ADDITIONAL APPLICATION

Goal Setting—With so many things expected of us, it's easy to feel overwhelmed. Without proper objectives (goals), we can sink fast. Carefully add the egg to the glass of water. As we set goals and accomplish them, we find that we are better able to cope with our responsibilities. Remove the egg and stir in a tablespoon of salt for each goal discussed. Replace the egg. Eventually we are "floating" instead of "sinking." D&C 103:36 states, "All victory and glory is brought to pass unto you through your diligence, faithfulness, and prayers of faith." If we are diligent and faithful in our goals, then we will be victorious in our righteous desires.

MAGNIFY YOUR CALLING

"And we did magnify our office unto the Lord." Jacob 1:19

THINGS YOU WILL NEED
Magnifying glass
Copy of quote listed below
Scriptures

EXPERIMENT
The magnifying glass is used to enlarge the print of a quote so that it can be read aloud to the class.

GOSPEL APPLICATION
In Jacob 1:18–19 we learn of the example that Jacob and his brother, Joseph, set in magnifying their callings. They taught the word of God with all diligence—laboring with all their might so that their garments would be found spotless at the last day. In the May 1986 issue of the Ensign, Thomas S. Monson told us what it means to magnify a calling. Have someone use the magnifying glass to read the quote below.

What does it mean to magnify a calling? It means to build it up in dignity and importance, to make it honorable and commendable in the eyes of all men, to enlarge and strengthen it, to let the light of heaven shine through it to the view of other men. And how does one magnify a calling? Simply by performing the service that pertains to it.
—Thomas S. Monson, "Priesthood Power," *New Era*, May 2001, 6

NO MAN CAN SERVE TWO MASTERS

"Ye cannot serve God and mammon." Matthew 6:24

THINGS YOU WILL NEED
Paper
Pencil or pen

EXPERIMENT
Invite a volunteer to come forward and give them the paper and pencil. Invite them to sit at a table and instruct them to write their name in cursive while at the same time moving one leg in a circular, clockwise pattern. When the volunteer is in the middle of writing their name, instruct them to change the direction of their leg circles to counterclockwise. They should get nothing more than unreadable scribbles.

GOSPEL APPLICATION
The concentration of the volunteer was broken when they tried to do both tasks at the same time. Often times, by our choices, we try to please God and the world. But as it states in Matthew 6:24, a person will either "hate the one, and love the other; or else he will hold to the one, and despise the other." We should make choices that keep our concentration on God and not be distracted by the things of the world.

NOURISHED BY THE WORD OF GOD

"And their names were taken, that they might be remembered and
nourished by the good word of God." Moroni 6:4

THINGS YOU WILL NEED
Two glasses of water
Salt
Spoon
Raisins or prunes

EXPERIMENT
Stir as much salt as possible into one of the glasses of water.
Drop a few raisins or prunes into each glass of water. Eventually
the fruit in the plain water will swell, while the fruit in the salt
water will not.

GOSPEL APPLICATION
We can liken this experiment to the words found in Alma
32:37–38. In these verses, the word of the Lord is represented
by a seed that has sprouted into a tree. If we nourish the tree, it
will take root, grow up, and bring forth good fruit. If we fail to
nourish the tree, it will not take root and will wither away.
Alma adds in verse 39, "Now, this is not because the seed was
not good, neither is it because the fruit thereof would not be
desirable; but it is because your ground is barren, and ye will
not nourish the tree, therefore ye cannot have the fruit
thereof." Are we like the glass of salt water—not allowing the
gospel to penetrate our lives and swell within us? Or are we like
the glass of plain water that nourishes the word of God and
allows it to swell?

ADDITIONAL APPLICATION

Bitterness of Sin—The glass of salt water represents a life filled with sin. As long as sin (salt) is present, the person (fruit) goes unnourished spiritually. On the other hand, if a person's life is free from sin, it is much easier to be spiritually fed. This is demonstrated by the way the pure water penetrates and swells the fruit.

OBEDIENCE

"Blessed are they that hear the word of God, and keep it."
Luke 11:28

THINGS YOU WILL NEED

Recipe for cookies of your choice
Plate of cookies made from the recipe
One or two burned cookies

EXPERIMENT

Display the plate of cookies, the recipe card, and the burned cookies.

GOSPEL APPLICATION

Isaiah 1:19 states, "If ye be willing and obedient, ye shall eat the good of the land." In order to receive blessings from Heavenly Father, we must be obedient to His commandments. D&C 130:20–21 states, "There is a law, irrevocably decreed in heaven before the foundations of this world, upon which all blessings are predicated—And when we obtain any blessing from God, it is by obedience to that law upon which it is predicated." Demonstrate this by showing the plate of cookies. In order to have success in baking the cookies, you had to follow the directions carefully. If the proper baking time is ignored, the cookies could burn. What happens to people who do not follow the directions given by the Lord? 3 Nephi 25:1 states, "For behold, the day cometh that shall burn as an oven; and all the proud, yea, and all that do wickedly, shall be stubble; and the day that cometh shall burn them up, saith the Lord of Hosts, that it shall leave them neither root nor branch."

OUR BODIES ARE TEMPLES

"Know ye not that ye are the temple of God, and that the Spirit of God dwelleth in you?" 1 Corinthians 3:16

THINGS YOU WILL NEED
Two clear glasses
Food coloring or ink
Two white carnations

EXPERIMENT
The preparation for this experiment needs to take place several hours (or one day) before the presentation. Place about an inch of water in one glass. Add food coloring or ink to the water. Trim the stems of the flowers to about 6" in length. Place one of the flowers in the colored water and let it sit for several hours. Place the other flower in the glass of regular water. Set it aside to be used during the presentation. As the first flower absorbs the colored water, the flower changes color.

GOSPEL APPLICATION
We learn in 1 Corinthians 3:16 that our bodies are temples in which the Spirit of God dwells. With that being the case, we need to treat our bodies with respect and be careful what we subject them to. In D&C 89, the Lord revealed to Joseph Smith words of wisdom on how we should treat our bodies. To show that what we put into our bodies does affect us, put a few drops of the food coloring or ink into the glass of clear water. Point out that even though the flower is white at the moment, it will slowly absorb the colored water and be affected both internally and externally. Demonstrate this concept by showing the previously prepared flower to the class. If we follow the counsel given us in the Word

of Wisdom and are respectful of our bodies, great blessings will be ours (refer to D&C 89:18–20).

ADDITIONAL APPLICATION

Morality—The people and things in our lives, such as our friends, our hobbies, our choices of movies, books, magazines, and TV shows, can greatly affect us. Whether we realize it or not, our surroundings can influence us for good or evil. If we choose to associate with friends who are contentious, unkind, or immoral, then we stand a greater risk of becoming the same way. Every time we expose ourselves to wickedness, we can absorb some of it and be affected by it. Demonstrate this by showing the two flowers. The flower in the colored water represents someone who has chosen to be surrounded by (and therefore absorb) unrighteousness. The flower in the clear water represents someone who has chosen to be surrounded by righteousness.

OUR POTENTIAL

"Ye are gods; and all of you are children of the most High."
Psalm 82:6

THINGS YOU WILL NEED
Balloon
Soft-drink bottle

EXPERIMENT
Place the uninflated balloon in the bottle with the open end of the balloon folded over the outside rim of the bottle's mouth. Hold the mouth of the bottle to your lips and try to blow up the balloon. It can't be done. But when you remove the restriction of the bottle, the ballon will blow up fine.

GOSPEL APPLICATION
Sometimes through fear and self-doubt we limit ourselves—preventing us from reaching our potential. The Lord tells us in Psalm 82:6, "Ye are gods; and all of you are children of the most High." With this knowledge, we can remove the fears and doubts that hold us back, and we can then reach our true potential.

OUTWARD APPEARANCE

"For the Lord seeth not as man seeth; for man looketh on the
outward appearance, but the Lord looketh on the heart."
1 Samuel 16:7

THINGS YOU WILL NEED
Blue or green food coloring
A carton of milk
Paper cups
Cookies (optional)

EXPERIMENT
Prior to the lesson, drop several drops of food coloring into
the carton of milk and stir. Close the carton.

GOSPEL APPLICATION
Offer cookies and milk to the class. (If you have a large
class, you might ask for just a few class members to come
forward and participate.) As you pour the milk into the cups,
some members may not want to partake because of the unusual
appearance of the milk—even though the milk's taste is not
affected. We learn from 1 Samuel 16:7 that "man looketh on
the outward appearance." If we want others to know that we
are followers of Christ, then our appearance needs to reflect
that—not only our outward appearance, but our words and
actions also. When our appearance does not reflect Christ, then
we will have a hard time converting others to His gospel. Just
as the appearance of the milk might discourage some partici-
pants from tasting it, the wrong outward appearance could
discourage some people from accepting the truthfulness of the
gospel.

ADDITIONAL APPLICATION

Judging Others—Offer several class members a glass of milk. As you pour it, some members may not be so eager to drink it. They may pre-judge the taste by its appearance. When it comes to judging others, we are warned in Moroni 7:18 to "not judge wrongfully; for with that same judgment which ye judge ye shall also be judged." We need to follow the example of the Lord, who "looketh on the heart" of the individual (1 Samuel 16:7). Since we do not have the ability to see a person's heart in the way the Lord does, we need to do all we can to get to know someone before we offer up judgment—and then only with "righteous judgment," as stated in John 7:24.

OVERCOMING THE WORLD

"He that is faithful and endureth shall overcome the world."
D&C 63:47

THINGS YOU WILL NEED
Ping-pong ball
Glass quart jar with lid
Wheat (to fill the jar)
Permanent marker

EXPERIMENT
Using a permanent marker, draw a face on the ping-pong ball. Place the ball in the jar. Fill the jar within 1 1/2" of the top with wheat. Put the lid on the jar and tighten. Turn the jar upside down and gently shake until the ping-pong ball comes to the surface.

GOSPEL APPLICATION
In John 16:33, Christ teaches us that we will have tribulations in this world. Place the ball in the jar and discuss various tribulations we may face. As each is mentioned, place a scoop of wheat on top of the ball. Continue until the ball is completely covered and the jar is filled to within 1 1/2" of the top. Place the lid on the jar and tighten. We also learn from the same scripture that we should be of good cheer because Christ overcame the world. If we are faithful and endure, we shall also overcome the world (see D&C 63:47). Turn the jar over and gently shake until the ball "overcomes" the wheat.

ADDITIONAL APPLICATION
Goal Setting—Many of the goals we set in life are not accomplished by one or two simple steps. Major goals are

accomplished by successfully completing several smaller goals. We can read about this in Mosiah 4:27: "And see that all these things are done in wisdom and order; for it is not requisite that a man should run faster than he has strength. And again, it is expedient that he should be diligent, that thereby he might win the prize; therefore, all things must be done in order." Place the ball in the jar and fill it with wheat to within 1 1/2" of the top. Secure the lid. Turn the jar over and demonstrate how things are accomplished one step at a time by gently shaking the jar—with each "shake" representing the accomplishment of one small goal. Continue until the ball comes out on top—symbolizing the accomplishment of a major goal.

OVERCOMING WEAKNESSES

"If [men] humble themselves before me, and have faith in me, then will I make weak things become strong unto them." Ether 12:27

THINGS YOU WILL NEED

A sheet of newspaper (about 12" x 18")

EXPERIMENT

Make a paper banger by following the instructions on the next page. Grip the banger by the two sharp corners. Flick it down quickly to make a loud bang.

GOSPEL APPLICATION

The sheet of newspaper appears to be weak and flimsy when held up for the class to see. But Heavenly Father has promised us that if we humble ourselves and have faith, He will make our weaknesses become strengths (see Ether 12:27). In D&C 35:13, we also learn that Heavenly Father calls upon the weak things of the world to "thrash the nations." Follow the instructions below to fold the newspaper into a paper banger. Grip the banger by the two sharp corners and flick it down sharply—demonstrating the strength and power of the once weak newspaper.

HOW TO MAKE A PAPER BANGER

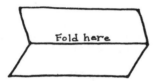

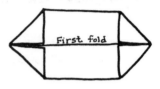

1. Fold the paper in half lengthways. Then open it out.

2. Fold each corner into the first fold.

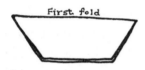

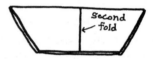

3. Fold the paper in half along the first fold. Fold it in half again.

4. Open out the second fold.

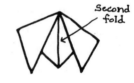

5. Fold the two outside corners down.

6. Fold the paper back along the second fold to make a triangle shape.

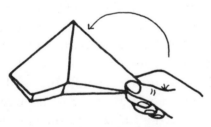

7. Grip the banger by the sharp corners. Flick it down quickly to make a loud bang.

PARENTAL RESPONSIBILITIES

"Train up a child in the way he should go: and when he is old, he
will not depart from it." Proverbs 22:6

THINGS YOU WILL NEED
Strong magnet
Four paper clips

EXPERIMENT
Suspend one paper clip from the magnet. Suspend the three
paper clips magnetically from the first clip (do not actually
hook the clips together). When the first clip is removed from
the magnet, most of the other clips fall.

GOSPEL APPLICATION
As parents, we have a responsibility to teach our children
the gospel through an example of righteous living. D&C
68:25 states, "And again, inasmuch as parents have children in
Zion, or in any of her stakes which are organized, that teach
them not to understand the doctrine of repentance, faith in
Christ the Son of the living God, and of baptism and the gift
of the Holy Ghost by the laying on of the hands, when eight
years old, the sin be upon the heads of the parents." Because of
their unrighteous living, the Nephites were warned by Jacob,
"Wherefore, ye shall remember your children, how that ye
have grieved their hearts because of the example that ye have
set before them; and also, remember that ye may, because of
your filthiness, bring your children unto destruction, and their
sins be heaped upon your heads at the last day" (Jacob 3:10).
The magnet represents the gospel. When we as parents "stay
connected" to the gospel through righteous living, our children have a better chance of staying connected. But if we fall

away and remove ourselves from the gospel, our children risk falling also.

ADDITIONAL APPLICATION

Blessings from the Lord—David said in Psalm 37:4, "Delight thyself also in the Lord; and he shall give thee the desires of thine heart." Moses said in Deuteronomy 28:2, "And all these blessings shall come on thee, and overtake thee, if thou shalt hearken unto the voice of the Lord thy God." The first paper clip represents us, the other clips represent the blessings given to us by hearkening unto the Lord. When we delight in the Lord and stay close to Him (the magnet), then it is our privilege to have blessings "attached" to our lives. But when we remove ourselves from the Lord, our blessings fall away.

THE POWER OF THE ATONEMENT

"And were it not for the atonement they must
unavoidably perish." Mosiah 13:28

THINGS YOU WILL NEED
Apple
Small knife
Small plate
Lemon

EXPERIMENT

A few hours before your lesson, cut the apple into four parts. Squeeze lemon juice onto two of the apple slices. Leave the other two apple slices untreated. After a few hours, the untreated slices will turn brown, while the treated slices will not.

GOSPEL APPLICATION

Show the class the two sets of apple slices. Explain that when an apple is cut open and exposed to air, it begins to brown unless it is treated. Two of the slices were left untreated and have begun to "perish." The other two are being preserved because of the treatment they were given. Mosiah 13:28 states, "were it not for the atonement, which God himself shall make for the sins and iniquities of his people, that they must unavoidably perish" Just as the apple slices were kept pure by the lemon treatment, the Atonement is the ultimate treatment for our lives to save us from perishing spiritually and physically.

PRAY ALWAYS

"Men ought always to pray, and not to faint." Luke 18:1

THINGS YOU WILL NEED
    Funnel with small opening
    Clear glass bottle
    Clay
    Water
    Straw

EXPERIMENT

Place the funnel into the bottle and, using the clay, make an airtight seal around the mouth of the bottle. Pour water into the funnel. It should not flow into the bottle. At the appropriate time, place your finger over one end of the straw and push the other end through the funnel. Lift your finger. The water will now flow into the bottle.

GOSPEL APPLICATION

D&C 19:38 states, "Pray always, and I will pour out my Spirit upon you, and great shall be your blessing." In order to receive blessings from Heavenly Father, we need to pray not just often, but also with real intent. Mormon states in Moroni 7:9, "And likewise also is it counted evil unto a man, if he shall pray and not with real intent of heart; yea, and it profiteth him nothing, for God receiveth none such." Demonstrate the importance of prayer in obtaining blessings by stating that the water represents blessings from Heavenly Father. When the "blessings" are poured into the funnel, they wait there until we do our part. The straw represents sincere prayer. When we apply "sincere prayer," the blessings are poured out upon us.

ADDITIONAL APPLICATIONS

Tithing—Malachi 3:10 states, "Bring ye all the tithes into the storehouse, that there may be meat in mine house, and prove me now herewith, saith the Lord of hosts, if I will not open you the windows of heaven, and pour you out a blessing, that there shall not be room enough to receive it." The water represents blessings from the Lord. The straw represents tithing. When we pay our tithing, we allow the Lord to pour out His blessings upon us.

Faith and Humility—D&C 105:12 states, "For behold, I have prepared a great endowment and blessing to be poured out upon them, inasmuch as they are faithful and continue in humility before me." The water represents blessings from the Lord. The straw represents faith and humilty. When we learn and apply these principles in our lives, we are worthy to have great blessings poured out upon us.

PRIORITIES

"To every thing there is a season, and a time to every purpose under the heaven." Ecclesiastes 3:1

THINGS YOU WILL NEED
Plastic spoon
Woolen cloth
Dish of puffed rice cereal

EXPERIMENT
Charge the plastic spoon by rubbing it with the woolen cloth. Hold the spoon over the dish of puffed rice and watch as the cereal jumps to the spoon then shoots off in different directions.

GOSPEL APPLICATION
"To every thing there is a season, and a time to every purpose under the heaven" (Ecclesiastes 3:1). When we try to do everything at once, we usually end up making a big mess. We need to set our priorities. We are taught in D&C 88:119, "Organize yourselves; prepare every needful thing; and establish a house, even a house of prayer, a house of fasting, a house of faith, a house of learning, a house of glory, a house of order, a house of God." If we learn to set our priorities, then we will have order and not confusion. Demonstrae this by picking up a few grains of cereal at a time using your fingers.

ADDITIONAL APPLICATIONS
Envy and Strife—James 3:16 states, "For where envying and strife is, there is confusion and every evil work." Demonstrate this by rubbing the spoon on the woolen cloth to represent envy and strife. The results will be wild confusion as

the puffed rice cereal shoots in every direstion. On the other hand, as we learn in verses 17–18, "The wisdom that is from above is first pure, then peaceable, gentle, and easy to be intreated, full of mercy and good fruits, without partiality, and without hypocrisy. And the fruit of righteousness is sown in peace of them that make peace." Hold a different spoon that has not been rubbed with the cloth over the rice. It should have a more "peaceable" result.

Gossip—The danger with gossiping is that once a story is told, you have no control of where it goes from there. Rub the spoon with the woolen cloth to represent the act of gossiping. Hold the spoon over the cereal and watch how the "story" flies out of control and in every direction.

PROTECTION FROM SIN

"But thou, O Lord, art a shield for me; my glory, and the lifter up of mine head." Psalm 3:3

THINGS YOU WILL NEED

    One hard-boiled egg
    White crayon
    One cup of white vinegar with
        food coloring added

EXPERIMENT
    Using the crayon, draw and color in the shape of a shield on the egg. Place the egg in the colored vinegar and let sit for a minute or so. When the egg is removed, the egg will be colored except for the area drawn with crayon.

GOSPEL APPLICATION
    Proverbs 30:5 states, "Every word of God is pure: he is a shield unto them that put their trust in him." The egg represents an individual, the crayon represents the word of God, and the colored vinegar represents sin. By following the commandments of God, we can be protected from sin just as the crayon protected the egg from the coloring.

PURIFICATION

"Wash thine heart from wickedness, that thou mayest be saved."
Jeremiah 4:14

THINGS YOU WILL NEED
    Clear glass jar with mud smeared on the inside
    Bottle brush
    Liquid dishwashing detergent
    Dish towel
    Tub or large bowl with water

EXPERIMENT
    First try to clean the jar by wiping only the outside. Then place soap and water in the jar and use the bottle brush to clean the inside. Rinse, then dry with a towel.

GOSPEL APPLICATION
    In Moroni's epistle to Pahoran he states, "Now I would that ye should remember that God has said that the inward vessel shall be cleansed first, and then shall the outer vessel be cleansed also" (Alma 60:23). The commandment to purify our hearts is found many times throughout the scriptures. Our hearts are the first thing we must cleanse if we are to become truly pure. To demonstrate the importance of cleansing the "inward vessel" first, try cleaning the jar by wiping the outside only. No matter how clean we get the outside, the inside is still dirty and shows through. Now wash the inside with soap and water. When the jar is cleansed from the inside, the outside is visibly improved.

PURITY

"Lay hold upon every good gift, and touch not the evil gift, nor the unclean thing." Moroni 10:30

THINGS YOU WILL NEED
Bowl of mud

EXPERIMENT
Challenge a class member to place their bare hands in the mud without getting muddy. It can't be done.

GOSPEL APPLICATION
Mormon exhorted us in Moroni 10:30 to "touch not the evil gift, nor the unclean thing." Paul taught us to "cleanse ourselves from all filthiness of the flesh and spirit" (2 Corinthians 7:1). Our world is full of movies, television shows, music, and activities that are covered with spiritual mud and filthiness. No matter what others say, participating in these things will affect us spiritually. As demonstrated, we just can't play in the mud without getting muddy!

ADDITIONAL APPLICATION
Repentance—Along with the bowl of mud, you will also need moist towelettes and a white dress or shirt for this experiment. The mud represents sin and the white clothing represents the kingdom of heaven. The moist towelettes represent repentance. Begin by placing your hands in the bowl of mud, then act like you're going to put on the white piece of clothing. Ask if it would be possible for you to put on the clothing without getting it dirty. Of course not. Ask someone to read 3 Nephi 27:19. It is impossible for any unclean thing to enter the kingdom of heaven. Ask someone to continue by reading verse

20. In order to stand spotless before God, we must repent. Demonstrate this by washing your hands with the moist towelettes. It may take some work to get your hands clean, just as it takes work to complete the process of repentance. If you cleanse yourself from all sin and endure to the end, you will be saved in the kingdom of heaven. Demonstrate this by putting on the white clothing with your clean hands.

PUTTING GOD FIRST

"Seek ye first the kingdom of God, and his righteousness; and all these things shall be added unto you." Matthew 6:33

THINGS YOU WILL NEED
Clear glass jar
Several small balls
Dry beans
Rice
Sugar
Small sealable plastic bags

EXPERIMENT

The various items, when placed in the jar in the proper order, fill the jar perfectly. If items are placed in the wrong order, they won't all fit.

GOSPEL APPLICATION

Before presenting this experiment, you may want to practice filling your jar with the various items until you know exactly how much the jar will hold when the items are put into it in the order of largest to smallest. Then put those quantities of the items into separate small plastic bags and seal the bags. If you wish, divide the quantity of sugar among two or three bags, depending on how many "lower priority" items you plan to discuss. Label the bag of balls "Prayer." Label the bag of beans "Scripture study." Label the bag of rice "Church attendance." Label the bags of sugar with various activities or tasks, such as work, hobbies, and recreation. Begin the experiment by placing the bags of sugar into the jar first, followed by the bags containing the larger items. Unfortunately, there won't be enough room for scriptures and prayers. Matthew 6:33 states, "But seek ye first the kingdom of

God, and his righteousness; and all these things shall be added unto you." If we put God first in our lives by having daily prayer and scripture study and attending all our Church meetings, then we will have adequate time to accomplish our other desires. Demonstrate this by removing all of the bags from the jar and then emptying the balls (prayer) from the plastic bag into the jar. Next, empty the bag of beans into the jar. Add the bag of rice (Church attendance), then the sugar (work, hobbies, recreation) into the jar until everything fits perfectly.

ADDITIONAL APPLICATION

Spiritual Feast—Matthew 5:6 says, "Blessed are they which do hunger and thirst after righteousness: for they shall be filled." We quench our hunger and thirst for righteousness by feasting upon spiritual things. In this experiment the bag of balls could be labeled "Prayer," the bag of beans could be labeled "Scripture study," the bag of rice could be labeled "Church attendance," and the bag of sugar could be labeled "Service to others." Empty the contents of the bags into the jar one at a time (starting with the largest items and ending with the smallest). After each addition it may appear there is no room left in the jar, but as each item is added, there continues to be room for spiritual food.

READY TO RECEIVE

"And there are none that doeth good except those who are ready to receive the fulness of my gospel" D&C 35:12

THINGS YOU WILL NEED
Two small-mouthed bottles
Very large funnel
Very small funnel
Large bowl
Pitcher of water

EXPERIMENT
Place the small funnel in the mouth of one of the bottles. Place the bottle in the center of the bowl. Quickly pour half the water into the small funnel, allowing much of it to spill over into the bowl. Remove the bottle from the bowl and set it aside. Place the large funnel in the mouth of the other bottle. Place the bottle in the bowl. Quickly pour the remaining water into the large funnel. Some of it will probably still spill into the bowl, but more water should end up in this bottle than the first bottle. Compare the water levels in the two bottles.

GOSPEL APPLICATION
Just as a teacher needs the Spirit to teach (see D&C 42:14) we also need the Spirit to learn. When we attend any Church meeting, we can only take away from it what we are willing and prepared to receive. When we seek the Spirit ahead of time through study and prayer, we are able to take in so much more of the message. The large funnel in the bottle represents someone who prepared ahead of time and therefore received more. On the other hand, our lack of preparation prevents us from receiving the whole message. The small funnel in the

bottle represents someone who failed to prepare ahead of time and therefore missed much of the message.

RECORD KEEPING

"Write the things which you have seen and heard." 3 Nephi 27:23

THINGS YOU WILL NEED
Paper and pencil for each class member

EXPERIMENT
Pass out the paper and pencils and challenge each class member to write down the events of any ordinary day that happened a year ago, six months ago, one month ago, and a week ago.

GOSPEL APPLICATION
When Christ visited the people of ancient America, He said unto Nephi, "Bring forth the record which ye have kept" (3 Nephi 23:7). Nephi did as the Lord requested. When Christ looked over the records, He saw that they were not complete—some important events had been left out. What would we do if Christ appeared to us and asked for our personal or family record? Would the records be complete? We can follow the Nephites' example of obedience by completing the records in our charge (see 3 Nephi 23:13).

REPELLING SIN

"Submit yourselves therefore to God. Resist the devil, and he will flee from you." James 4:7

THINGS YOU WILL NEED
Bowl of water
Pepper
Small bar of soap (preferably heart-shaped)
Teaspoon of sugar

EXPERIMENT
Sprinkle some pepper into the bowl of water. Dipping the soap into the water will repel the pepper. Sprinkling the sugar into the water will attract the pepper.

GOSPEL APPLICATION
In this experiment, the pepper represents sin, the sugar represents unrighteous living, and the soap represents righteous living. Sprinkle the pepper into the water—representing sin and unrighteousness. If we make righteous choices and have a pure heart, we will then repel sin. As stated in James 4:7, "Submit yourselves therefore to God. Resist the devil, and he will flee from you." Demonstrate this principle by dipping the soap into the water and watching the pepper flee to the sides of the bowl. When the sugar is sprinkled onto the water, the pepper is drawn towards the sugar. Explain that unrighteous living and choices will attract sin. Place the soap into the water once again so that you end the experiment with the sin "fleeing" from you.

ADDITIONAL APPLICATIONS
Kind Words—Proverbs 15:1 says, "A soft answer turneth away wrath: but grievous words stir up anger." Perform the

experiment with the soap representing the harshness of grievous words, the sugar representing the sweetness of kind words, and the pepper representing those around us. When we use grievous words, people around us want to flee. When we use kind words, people are drawn to us.

Repentance—In Ezekiel 18:30 we are counseled, "Repent, and turn yourselves from all your trangressions; so iniquity shall not be your ruin." The pepper represents sin (or mistakes), while the soap represents repentance. When we repent, we turn away from our sins and become clean again. Demonstrate this by placing the soap in the water. Sometimes after we repent, we make mistakes again. Demonstrate this by sprinkling the sugar onto the surface of the water. As the pepper (mistakes) return, ask the class how often they can repent and be forgiven. To find the answer, have someone read Moroni 6:8 aloud. Place the soap in the water once again and watch as the sin is turned away and the person is cleansed once again.

RESISTING TEMPTATION

"Be faithful, and yield to no temptation." D&C 9:13

THINGS YOU WILL NEED
Paintbrush
Iodine
Small jar with water
Small bowl
Lemon (or lemon juice)
White paper

EXPERIMENT
Squeeze some lemon juice into the bowl. Using the paintbrush, write "Let us resist evil" (Alma 61:14) in lemon juice on the paper. If desired, draw in lemon juice a simple crown at the bottom of the paper. Let the lemon juice dry. Place a few drops of iodine in the jar of water. Brush the paper with the iodine mixture. The paper will turn purple, but the scripture message will stay white.

GOSPEL APPLICATION
Moroni warns us to "be wise . . . that ye will yield to no temptation" (Mormon 9:28). We also learn in 1 Corinthians 10:13 that "God . . . will not suffer you to be tempted above that ye are able; but will with the temptation also make a way to escape, that ye may be able to bear it." How do we escape temptation? The answer can be found in 1 Nephi 15:24: "Whoso would hearken unto the word of God, and would hold fast unto it, they would never perish; neither could the temptations and the fiery darts of the adversary overpower them unto blindness, to lead them away to destruction." Alma's counsel to his son Helaman teaches us to have faith in Christ; to be humble,

meek, and lowly in heart; to never be weary of good works; and to learn wisdom in our youth and keep the commandments of God. We should counsel with the Lord in all our doings and pray to Him always. By doing all these things, we will have the strength we need to resist the temptations that surround us. (see Alma 37:33–37.) Brush the iodine onto the paper, explaining that the paper represents us, and the iodine represents temptation. By resisting temptation, we will receive the blessing found in James 1:12: "Blessed is the man that endureth temptation: for when he is tried, he shall receive the crown of life, which the Lord hath promised to them that love him."

ADDITIONAL APPLICATION

Keep the Sabbath Day Holy—Prior to class, write the words "Keep thyself unspotted from the world" in lemon juice on the paper. Let the lemon juice dry. With the class, discuss various ways to keep the Sabbath day holy (refer to D&C 59:10–13). As you brush the iodine onto the paper, have someone read D&C 59:9 aloud. The iodine represents wordly influences. The white writing represents our commitment to keeping the Sabbath day holy—we are unspotted from the world. By honoring the Sabbath, the Lord has promised us both temporal and spiritual blessings (refer to D&C 59:14–19). In contrast, you could brush some iodine onto paper that has not been previously written on with lemon juice. This could represent someone who is not keeping the commandments of the Lord and is spiritually blinded by the influences of the world.

RESURRECTION

"They can die no more; their spirits uniting with their bodies,
never to be divided." Alma 11:45

THINGS YOU WILL NEED
Clear glass jar with tight-fitting lid
Clear container of water
Clear container of oil
Egg

EXPERIMENT
Display the water, oil, and egg on a table. At the appropriate time in the presentation, place equal parts of water and oil in the jar, leaving a small amount of room at the top of the jar. Fasten the lid tightly. During the presentation, shake the jar then allow it to sit. Add the egg, shake, and allow it to sit again.

GOSPEL APPLICATION
Our spirit enters our body at the beginning of our earthly life and continues to dwell there until death. Demonstrate this by adding the oil (the spirit) to the water (the body) and shaking (life). At death, our spirit separates from the body. This is represented by letting the mixture sit until separated. Our spirit and body remain in this state of separation until the Resurrection. Speaking of the Resurrection, Alma said, "I say unto you that this mortal body is raised to an immortal body, that is from death, even from the first death unto life, that they can die no more; their spirits uniting with their bodies, never to be divided; thus the whole becoming spiritual and immortal, that they can no more see corruption" (Alma 11:45). Demonstrate this by adding the egg (representing new life) to

the oil and water. Shake and let sit. This time the oil (the spirit) and the water (the body) do not separate.

Note: There may be some foam that accumulates at the top after shaking, but the oil and water won't separate. To get rid of the foam, pour the mixture gently back and forth between two containers.

RIGHTEOUS JUDGMENT

"Judge not according to the appearance, but judge righteous judgment." John 7:24

THINGS YOU WILL NEED
A photocopy of the illustration, or a similar one you make yourself

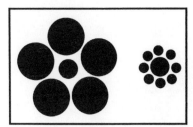

EXPERIMENT
Show the class the illustration and ask, "Which of the two middle circles is larger?" They will most likely chose the one on the right, but in reality, the two circles are the same size. They give the illusion of being different in size because we subconsciously judge them by the surrounding circles.

GOSPEL APPLICATION
Often times we judge others by what we think we see, or by their apparent surroundings. By doing so, we can sometimes misjudge them. Matthew 7:2 states, "For with what judgment ye judge, ye shall be judged: and with what measure ye mete, it shall be measured to you again." We should judge carefully and always seek to do so righteously.

ADDITIONAL APPLICATION
Avoiding the Appearance of Evil—1 Thessalonians 5:22 teaches, "Abstain from all appearance of evil." Whether we like it or not, we are often judged by our surroundings or who we associate with. We would be wise to follow the counsel given in D&C 87:8, which states, "Wherefore, stand ye in holy places, and be not moved." By standing in holy places, we can avoid the appeareance of evil and be judged accordingly.

SALVATION

"Work out your own salvation with fear and trembling."
Philippians 2:12

THINGS YOU WILL NEED
Pencil

EXPERIMENT
Invite a volunteer to come forward and make a loose fist, with their pinky downward. Hold the pencil just above the slightly open fist of the volunteer. Instruct them to catch the falling pencil by closing their hand as it falls. Unless they try to anticipate when you will drop it and close their fist prematurely, the reaction time of the brain to the hand will make it difficult, if not impossible, for them to catch it. Next, instruct the volunteer to hold the pencil just over their own fist and catch the pencil as they drop it. They should be able to catch it easily.

GOSPEL APPLICATION
Although the Atonement of Jesus Christ saves us from sin and provides for us a way to return to Heavenly Father, it is still up to us to apply the Atonement in our lives and "work out [our] own salvation with fear and trembling" (Philippians 2:12). We cannot depend on the good works of others to save us. The pencil represents the individual's salvation. If someone else tries to catch it, they fail. But, when the individual is responsible for their own salvation, they succeed.

SATAN DECEIVES

"And he became Satan . . . the father of all lies, to deceive and to blind men, and to lead them captive at his will." Moses 4:4

THINGS YOU WILL NEED
Newspaper
12" ruler

EXPERIMENT
Place the ruler at the edge of a table and let it extend about 5 inches past the edge. Unfold a single sheet of newspaper and lay it over the part of the ruler that is on the table. Bring your fist down sharply on the free end of the ruler. The air pressure on the newspaper will resist the blow made with your fist. It might even snap the ruler in half without tearing the newspaper.

GOSPEL APPLICATION
This experiment looks deceiving. How can the newspaper hold the ruler down, allowing it to be snapped in two? Most people would believe that the newspaper would tear before the ruler was snapped. This is similar to the way Satan works his deceitfulness. A description of Satan is found in Moses 4:4: "And he became Satan, yea, even the devil, the father of all lies, to deceive and to blind men, and to lead them captive at his will, even as many as would not hearken unto my voice." Nephi warns us in 2 Nephi 28:7 that "there shall be many which shall say: Eat, drink, and be merry, for tomorrow we die; and it shall be well with us." In verse 8 he also warns that many will justify committing a little sin, to lie a little and take advantage of others—with the belief that God will only beat them "with a few stripes," and then they will be saved in the kingdom of

God. This is exactly what Satan wants us to believe. We need to be aware of the devastating effects of sin. 1 John 1:8 warns, "If we say that we have no sin, we deceive ourselves, and the truth is not in us." Demonstrate this by using the ruler to represent an individual and the newspaper to represent their sins. The sins may not look as if they are holding the individual down, but in reality they are. Prove it by sharply striking the free end of the ruler with your fist. The ruler should resist your blow, or even break in half without tearing the newspaper.

SATAN'S INFLUENCE

"And he became Satan, yea, even the devil, the father of all lies, to deceive and to blind men." Moses 4:4

THINGS YOU WILL NEED
Two plastic bags
Narrow wooden stick (approx. 18" long)
Thumbtack with flat head
Vinegar
Baking soda
Drinking glass

EXPERIMENT
Place the plastic bags at each end of the stick. Place the thumbtack at the corner of a table with the point facing up. Carefully balance the stick on the tack. Pour some baking soda and vinegar into a glass. As it begins to fizz, carefully tilt the glass over one of the bags. The gas produced is heavier than air and should make the balance uneven.

GOSPEL APPLICATION
The New Testament speaks of Jesus healing those "that were oppressed of the devil" (Acts 10:38). We may not be able to see the devil or his followers, but their influence can weigh heavily upon us. Demonstrate this by showing how the invisible gas in the plastic bag weighs it down and makes the balance uneven. We must always guard against Satan's "invisible" tactics.

SHARING TALENTS

"To every man is given a gift by the Spirit of God . . . that all may
be profited thereby." D&C 46:11–12

THINGS YOU WILL NEED
Frying pan
Six eating utensils
Tape
String

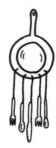

EXPERIMENT
Set one utensil aside, and then tie a 12"–18" piece of string
to each of the five remaining utensils. At the appropriate time
in the presentation, tape the end of each string inside the frying
pan as shown above. Strike the hanging utensils with the extra
utensil to produce a pleasing sound.

GOSPEL APPLICATION
D&C 46:11–12 states, "For all have not every gift given
unto them; for there are many gifts, and to every man is given a
gift by the Spirit of God. To some is given one, and to some is
given another, that all may be profited thereby." To demonstrate
this principle, hand out the utensils to various class members,
stating a talent that each possesses. Their individual talents may
be exceptional, but unless shared, they profit no one. When
brought together, talents can be magnified and enjoyed by all.
Ask the class members to come forward with their "talents" and
tape them to the inside bottom of the frying pan. Hold the
frying pan in the air and make a lovely sound by striking the
utensils.

ADDITIONAL APPLICATION

Faith without Works—We may have faith that the utensils can make a beautiful sound when united together, but if we don't apply the "works" by attaching them to the frying pan, our faith will be in vain. James 2:17 states, "Even so faith, if it hath not works, is dead, being alone." We continue to learn in verse 24, "Ye see then how that by works a man is justified, and not by faith only."

SHATTERED IMAGE

"A talebearer revealeth secrets: but he that is of a faithful spirit concealeth the matter." Proverbs 11:13

THINGS YOU WILL NEED
Two inexpensive hand mirrors (framed with metal or plastic)
Heavy paper sack
Hammer
Glass cleaner
Soft cloth

EXPERIMENT
Place one of the mirrors in the paper sack and close it tightly. At the appropriate time, carefully crack the mirror (while in the sack) with the hammer. Later in the demonstration, clean and shine the other mirror with glass cleaner.

GOSPEL APPLICATION
Ask a class member to come forward and look in the mirror. Comment on the perfect image that reflects from the mirror. Now place the mirror in the paper sack and carefully hit it with the hammer. Pull the mirror from the sack and have the class member look again at their reflection. This time the image is imperfect. No matter how hard we try, the image cannot be restored to its original state. This is similar to the effects of gossip. When we speak evil of others, we shatter their image—making restoration impossible. Paul taught the Ephesians, "Let no corrupt communication proceed out of your mouth, but that which is good to the use of edifying, that it may minister grace unto the hearers" (Ephesians 4:29). This advice is still true today. Instead of shattering someone's image by gossiping, we

can help to polish their image by using words that edify and uplift them. Demonstrate this by polishing the other mirror using the glass cleaner and soft cloth. Ask the class member to look into the polished mirror—commenting on the perfect image that is reflected.

ADDITIONAL APPLICATION

The Final Judgment—When speaking of the Final Judgment Alma said, "And it is requisite with the justice of God that men should be judged according to their works; and if their works were good in this life, and the desires of their hearts were good, that they should also, at the last day, be restored unto that which is good" (Alma 41:3). On the other hand, "If their works are evil they shall be restored unto them for evil" (Alma 41:4). Will our works on this earth cause our eternal reflection to be cracked and distorted, or beautifully polished? Have class members take turns viewing themselves in each mirror.

SINS REVEALED

"But behold, ye cannot hide your crimes from God." Alma 39:8

THINGS YOU WILL NEED
White paper
Milk
Small paintbrush
Iron

EXPERIMENT
Using the small paintbrush and milk, write various sins on the white paper. As the milk dries, the writing should become almost invisible. During the presentation, heat the iron and run it over the paper. The writing should now appear.

GOSPEL APPLICATION
Many people are under the false impression that they can hide their sins from the Lord. The Lord says in Jeremiah 16:17, "For mine eyes are upon all their ways: they are not hid from my face, neither is their iniquity hid from mine eyes." Alma 39:8 states, "But behold, ye cannot hide your crimes from God; and except ye repent they will stand as a testimony against you at the last day." We may be able to hide our sins from others, but God knows our sins and they are recorded. When the Lord comes again, He will "bring to light the hidden things of darkness, and will make manifest the counsels of the hearts" (1 Corinthians 4:5). Demonstrate this by running the iron over the paper to reveal the hidden sins.

ADDITIONAL APPLICATIONS
Service to Others—In the Sermon on the Mount, Jesus taught that we should do our service to others in secret. When

we do this, Heavenly Father will reward us openly (see Matthew 6:1–4). Use the paintbrush and milk to write various acts of service on the white paper. When the milk is dry, use the iron to reveal these secret acts.

Pray in Secret—In the Sermon on the Mount, Jesus taught that we should pray in secret. When we do so, Heavenly Father rewards us openly (Matthew 6:5–6). Use the paintbrush and milk to write Matthew 6:6 (or at least part of it) on the white paper. When the milk is dry, use the iron to represent how our secret prayers are known to God.

SMALL ACTS OF SERVICE

"And out of small things proceedeth that which is great."
D&C 64:33

THINGS YOU WILL NEED
Five or six marbles
Flat ruler with groove down the center

EXPERIMENT
Place the ruler flat on the table. Place all but one of the marbles on the groove of the ruler close enough that they are touching each other. Roll the extra marble against the line of marbles on the ruler. The marble at the opposite end will roll away.

GOSPEL APPLICATION
D&C 64:33 states, "Be not weary in well-doing, for ye are laying the foundation of a great work. And out of small things proceedeth that which is great." Sometimes we may feel like our small acts of service are not helping, but according to the demonstration, we never know the effect they have on the other end.

ADDITIONAL APPLICATION
Gossip—The spreading of stories at one end can affect someone at the other end—usually in an adverse way.
Good Works—Galations 6:7 states, "For whatsoever a man soweth, that shall he also reap." If we sow good works all our days, then we shall reap the same. The demonstration shows that one marble "reaps" one marble at the other end. Two marbles rolled into the line of marbles "reaps" two marbles at the other end. Three "reaps" three, and so on.

SMALL THINGS

"And out of small things proceedeth that which is great."
D&C 64:33

THINGS YOU WILL NEED

1 or 2 photocopies of the following page—enough so that you'll have a copy of the scripture verse for each student

Index cards with a pin hole in the center of each—one for each student

EXPERIMENT

Give each student a copy of the scripture along with a previously prepared card. At the appropriate time, have them hold the cards close to their eyes and look through them. As they bring the scripture verse closer to the card, they will be able to clearly read the fine print.

GOSPEL APPLICATION

The Lord has told us to "be not weary in well-doing" because "out of small things proceedeth that which is great" (D&C 64:33). Instruct the students to bring the cards close to their eyes as you explain that sometimes we may feel that our efforts are small and insignificant like the small hole in the card. But just as the small hole has the power to magnify the text, the Lord has the power to magnify our efforts and turn them into great things. Invite the students to read the "magnified" scripture verse. The Lord notices all our good works, no matter how small, for "by very small means the Lord doth confound the wise and bringeth about the salvation of many souls" (Alma 37:7.)

"Wherefore, be not weary in well-doing,
for ye are laying the foundation of a great work.
And out of small things proceedeth that which is great."
D&C 64:33

"Wherefore, be not weary in well-doing,
for ye are laying the foundation of a great work.
And out of small things proceedeth that which is great."
D&C 64:33

"Wherefore, be not weary in well-doing,
for ye are laying the foundation of a great work.
And out of small things proceedeth that which is great."
D&C 64:33

"Wherefore, be not weary in well-doing,
for ye are laying the foundation of a great work.
And out of small things proceedeth that which is great."
D&C 64:33

"Wherefore, be not weary in well-doing,
for ye are laying the foundation of a great work.
And out of small things proceedeth that which is great."
D&C 64:33

"Wherefore, be not weary in well-doing,
for ye are laying the foundation of a great work.
And out of small things proceedeth that which is great."
D&C 64:33

"Wherefore, be not weary in well-doing,
for ye are laying the foundation of a great work.
And out of small things proceedeth that which is great."
D&C 64:33

"Wherefore, be not weary in well-doing,
for ye are laying the foundation of a great work.
And out of small things proceedeth that which is great."
D&C 64:33

"Wherefore, be not weary in well-doing,
for ye are laying the foundation of a great work.
And out of small things proceedeth that which is great."
D&C 64:33

"Wherefore, be not weary in well-doing,
for ye are laying the foundation of a great work.
And out of small things proceedeth that which is great."
D&C 64:33

"Wherefore, be not weary in well-doing,
for ye are laying the foundation of a great work.
And out of small things proceedeth that which is great."
D&C 64:33

"Wherefore, be not weary in well-doing,
for ye are laying the foundation of a great work.
And out of small things proceedeth that which is great."
D&C 64:33

"Wherefore, be not weary in well-doing,
for ye are laying the foundation of a great work.
And out of small things proceedeth that which is great."
D&C 64:33

"Wherefore, be not weary in well-doing,
for ye are laying the foundation of a great work.
And out of small things proceedeth that which is great."
D&C 64:33

"Wherefore, be not weary in well-doing,
for ye are laying the foundation of a great work.
And out of small things proceedeth that which is great."
D&C 64:33

"Wherefore, be not weary in well-doing,
for ye are laying the foundation of a great work.
And out of small things proceedeth that which is great."
D&C 64:33

"Wherefore, be not weary in well-doing,
for ye are laying the foundation of a great work.
And out of small things proceedeth that which is great."
D&C 64:33

"Wherefore, be not weary in well-doing,
for ye are laying the foundation of a great work.
And out of small things proceedeth that which is great."
D&C 64:33

SOFT ANSWERS

"A soft answer turneth away wrath: but grievous words stir up anger." Proverbs 15:1

THINGS YOU WILL NEED
Two balloons
Two pieces of string
(each about 24" long)
A woolen cloth
Permanent marker

EXPERIMENT

Blow up both balloons and tie a string to each. Write the words "Soft Answers" on each balloon. Hold the balloons by the strings and let them hang down. They should be attracted to each other. Later in the experiment, cross out the words "Soft Answers" and replace them with a variety of insulting or "grievous" words. Rub the balloons on the woolen cloth and then allow them to hang down from the strings again. They should now repel each other.

GOSPEL APPLICATION

Proverbs 15:1 teaches us about the power of words. When we use kind words, they turn away wrath and invite a sense of calmness. When we use grievous words, on the other hand they have the opposite effect. These types of words can upset others and create a feeling of hostility. James chapter 3 explains the importance of bridling our tongue and not speaking evil of others. When we learn to speak without offending others, we become more perfect.

SOFTENED BY AFFLICTIONS

"Many were softened because of their afflictions, insomuch that they did humble themselves before God." Alma 62:41

THINGS YOU WILL NEED
Two hard-boiled eggs
One cup of vinegar

EXPERIMENT
One week prior to presenting this experiment, place one of the hard-boiled eggs in the cup of vinegar and allow it to sit for a week. This will allow the shell to become softened. Immediately prior to the presentation, remove the egg, rinse, and pat dry. Allow both eggs (still in their shells) to be passed around the class during the presentation.

GOSPEL APPLICATION
We read in Alma 62:41, "But behold, because of the exceedingly great length of the war between the Nephites and the Lamanites many had become hardened, because of the exceedingly great length of the war; and many were softened because of their afflictions, insomuch that they did humble themselves before God, even in the depth of humility." When faced with afflictions, do we blame God for our troubles—allowing ourselves to become hardened like the regular hard-boiled egg? Or, do we allow the afflictions to soften and humble us like the vinegar-soaked egg?

SPIRITUAL DIFFERENCES

"For man looketh on the outward appearance, but the Lord looketh on the heart." 1 Samuel 16:7

THINGS YOU WILL NEED
   Pineapple
   Coconut
   Apple
   Other fruit, if desired
   Basket (optional)

EXPERIMENT

   Display the basket of fruit on the table in view of the class. During the presentation, each fruit will be compared to the others.

GOSPEL APPLICATION

   Point out to the class that each piece of fruit is similar in that they are all fruit, but they have different qualities and different exteriors. We too are all similar to each other in that we are all children of God, but we have different qualities, exteriors, and levels of spirituality. We each have a precious spirit inside; some are buried deep within and harder to get to, while some are close to the surface. Demonstrate this by comparing the different surfaces of the fruit. It is easy to enjoy the tender fruit of the apple, because its skin is quite thin. A pineapple is a different story, however. Its skin is rough and prickly, making it more difficult to enjoy the sweet fruit within. A coconut is nearly impossible to open. Extra tools are needed to enjoy its contents. When we view others, we need to remember that everyone has something wonderful inside, even if the exterior is a little hard to get through.

SPIRITUAL GIFTS

"There are many gifts, and to every man is given a gift by the Spirit of God." D&C 46:11

THINGS YOU WILL NEED
Scissors
Clear blue, yellow, and red plastic sheets
A white surface

EXPERIMENT
Cut each of the clear colored sheets into several strips of equal widths. When the strips are placed on the white surface individually, they only reflect their individual color. When the strips overlap each other, they create new colors.

GOSPEL APPLICATION
In D&C 46:11–12, we learn the following facts about spiritual gifts: that there are many gifts of the Spirit given to man; not every gift is given to every man; each man is given at least one gift; and that these gifts are given so that "all may be profited thereby." Invite three people to come forward. Give the red strips to one person, the yellow strips to another, and the blue strips to the last. Explain that these strips are symbolic of spiritual gifts. Ask the volunteers to place their set of strips in individual piles on the white surface. If these gifts continue to lie dormant, they profit no one. Now ask the individuals to take turns placing their strips on the white surface, letting the strips overlap at 90° angles—forming a pattern of squares (see illustration). As the strips overlap, they create new colors, providing diversity and beauty. This is the same with our spiritual gifts. If we use them properly, others will benefit from the diversity and beauty of the various gifts that are available to Heavenly Father's children.

ADDITIONAL APPLICATION

Talents—Each of us has been blessed with individual talents or gifts. We learn from Moroni 10:18 that these "good" gifts come from Christ. We need to use and improve these talents so that we will be given more (see D&C 82:18). Demonstrate this by giving an individual three "talents" (a stack of blue, a stack of yellow, and a stack of red strips). Invite the person to lay the strips on the white surface in a criss-cross pattern. As the strips overlap each other, they create new colors—representing the new talents we can discover when we use the talents we already know we have. The scriptures also warn us that we can lose our God-given talents if we don't use them (see D&C 60:2–3).

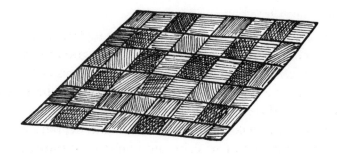

SPIRITUAL NOURISHMENT

"That they might be remembered and nourished by the good word
of God, to keep them in the right way." Moroni 6:4

THINGS YOU WILL NEED
Large bowl of water
Sponge

EXPERIMENT

Dip the sponge into the water. Hold the sponge over the
bowl and squeeze the water from the sponge a little at a time.
Refer to the lesson for further instructions.

GOSPEL APPLICATION

When preaching the Sermon on the Mount, Jesus taught
"Blessed are they which do hunger and thirst after righteousness: for they shall be filled" (Matthew 5:6). Attending Church
services each Sunday is one way to quench our thirst for righteousness. Dip the sponge into the water. As we go about our
week, various things will put a drain on our spirituality. Squeeze
the sponge a little at a time as you discuss things that might
drain our spirituality. If we do nothing about replenishing our
spirituality during the week, we could be completely drained by
the following Sunday, when we once again have the opportunity
to replenish our spiritual reservoir. But, if we truly "hunger and
thirst after righteousness," we will counteract the things that
drain us by replenishing our spiritual reservoirs during the
week. Discuss as a class various things that could replenish us,
such as scripture study, prayer, and service to others. With the
sponge, alternate squeezing a little and dipping a little to
symbolize the draining and replenishing that occurs during the
week. By always replenishing our spiritual reservoir, we will

maintain a healthy level of spirituality and not be left completely drained come Sunday.

ADDITIONAL APPLICATION

Parental Responsibility—For this experiment you will need one bowl of clear water, one bowl of dark-colored water, and two light-colored sponges. As parents, we have been commanded to bring up our children in light and truth (see D&C 93:40). Children learn by example and soak up everything—similar to a sponge. Dip the sponge into the clear water. This represents a child soaking up examples of truth and light. Jacob warned the Nephites that the bad example they set might bring destruction to their children, and that they would be held accountable for the sins of their children (see Jacob 3:10). If we set a bad example for our children, we will likewise be held accountable for their sins. Dip the sponge into the darkened water. This represents a child soaking up the bad example set by parents. We should all strive to set examples of truth and light to assure our children the best possible chance of returning to live with Heavenly Father.

SPIRITUAL STRENGTH

"Then will I make weak things become strong unto them."
Ether 12:27

THINGS YOU WILL NEED
Rope
Two dowels or broomsticks

EXPERIMENT
Invite two volunteers to come forward. Give each volunteer a stick and have them stand a few feet apart and face each other. Tie the end of the rope around one of the sticks, and weave the rope in and around the sticks as shown in the illustration. Ask the volunteers to pull the sticks apart as hard as they can while you pull on the loose end of the rope. No matter how hard they pull, you should be able to pull them together.

GOSPEL APPLICATION
The Lord has promised us in Ether 12:27 that if we humble ourselves before Him and have faith, He will make our weak things become strong. Before you place the rope around the sticks, try to pull the sticks together with your hands while the volunteers try hard to pull them apart, demonstrating your "weakness." Ask the class what a person could do to show humility and faith. While these suggestions are being discussed, wrap the rope around the sticks as shown. Ask the volunteers to pull the sticks apart again while you pull on the rope, demonstrating your "strength." Heavenly Father blesses us with spiritual strength when we put our trust in Him.

SPREADING THE GOSPEL

"Go ye into all the world, and preach the gospel to every creature."
Mark 16:15

THINGS YOU WILL NEED
Milk (not skim)
Bowl or saucer
Food coloring
Toothpick
Liquid dish soap

EXPERIMENT
Pour the milk into the bowl or saucer. Carefully a few drops of food coloring into the milk. Do not stir. Dip the toothpick in the liquid soap, then into the drops of food coloring. The food coloring will spread out to the sides of the container.

GOSPEL APPLICATION
Proclaiming the gospel is part of the three-fold mission of the Church. After His resurrection, Christ taught His apostles to "Go ye into all the world, and preach the gospel to every creature" (Mark 16:15). We also need to do our part in spreading the gospel. In this experiment the food coloring dropped into the milk represents the gospel. When the toothpick is dipped in soap and then dipped into the drops of food coloring, this represents those individuals who are willing to share their testimonies with others. Just as the food coloring spreads throughout the milk, the gospel is spread throughout the world by those willing to share.

ADDITIONAL APPLICATION
Gossiping—In D&C 42:27, we are commanded not to speak evil of our neighbor. The scriptures are full of warnings

against gossiping, backbiting, malice, and slander. When we spread a rumor about someone, there is really no way to correct the damage we cause. We can say that we are sorry and ask for forgiveness, but the story has still been told, and the damage is still there. This is demonstrated by the way the food coloring (stories) is spread throughout the milk by the soap-covered toothpick (a person who gossips). There is no way to reverse the process and have the food coloring return to the way it was, just as a story, once told, cannot be retrieved again.

STAY CLOSE TO THE GOSPEL

"Whoso would hearken unto the word of God, and would hold fast unto it, they would never perish." 1 Nephi 15:24

THINGS YOU WILL NEED
Paper clip
Strong magnet
Piece of thread, about 18" long
Tape

EXPERIMENT
Tie one end of the thread to the paper clip. Tape the other end to the table. Lift the clip with the magnet. If the magnet is pulled away too far, the clip will fall.

GOSPEL APPLICATION
In this experiment, the paper clip represents man and the magnet represents the gospel. When we live close to the gospel by obedience to the commandments of God, we are supported. But if we stray too far, we fall. We are warned in Proverbs 11:14 that "Where no counsel is, the people fall." We also learn in 1 Corinthians 10:12 that no matter who a man is and what level he is in the gospel, he should "take heed lest he fall." It is critical that we stay close to the gospel teachings so that we can be supported and strengthened in our journey to exaltation.

ADDITIONAL APPLICATION
Beware of Pride—Alma counsels his son Shiblon in Alma 38:11 not to be lifted up in pride or boast of his own wisdom and strength. Many times throughout the history of the Book of Mormon, the downfall of the people can be attributed to pride. The Lord promises in 2 Nephi 12:12 that the day will

come when the "proud and lofty," and all who are lifted up "shall be brought low." Demonstrate this by having the paper clip represent man and the magnet represent pride. The more the "pride" is raised, the higher the "man" is lifted. Eventually the pride will become so "lifted up" that the man will fall and be humbled. We understand the importance of humility by reading 2 Nephi 9:42, which states: "And whoso knocketh, to him will he open; and the wise, and the learned, and they that are rich, who are puffed up because of their learning, and their wisdom, and their riches—yea, they are they whom he despiseth; and save they shall cast these things away, and consider themselves fools before God, and come down in the depths of humility, he will not open unto them."

STRENGTH IN UNITY

"Be perfectly joined together in the same mind and in the same judgment." 1 Corinthians 1:10

THINGS YOU WILL NEED
Two yardsticks
Tape measure
Two clamps
Two chairs
String with heavy weight attached

EXPERIMENT
Set the two chairs back to back, about two and a half feet apart. Place the yardsticks across the backs of the chairs, one stick on top of the other. Tie the weight to the center of the sticks and allow it to hang down without touching the ground. Measure the distance between the low point of the sticks and the floor to see how much bending has taken place. Next, clamp the sticks together at each end and replace them on the backs of the chairs. Allow the weight to hang down once more, and measure the distance again. The sticks will bend less this time, because they are unified and strengthened by the clamps.

GOSPEL APPLICATION
Paul taught the Corinthians to "be perfectly joined together in the same mind and in the same judgment" (1 Corinthians 1:10). When, as a group, we have a task to complete, we will find more strength to finish the project when we are unified in mind and purpose. This is demonstrated by the yardsticks bending less when clamped together in unity.

ADDITIONAL APPLICATION

A Second Witness—Start with only one yardstick, and explain that on its own, the Bible is subject to many interpretations by many people. The principles can be "bent" according to the ideas of the person interpreting. Add the second yardstick and clamp the two together. Explain that when you add the Book of Mormon, you give strength to the principles taught in the Bible, and less bending occurs. The Lord says in Ezekial 37:16–17, "Moreover, thou son of man, take thee one stick, and write upon it, For Judah, and for the children of Israel his companions: then take another stick, and write upon it, For Joseph, the stick of Ephraim, and for all the house of Israel his companions: And join them one to another into one stick; and they shall become one in thine hand."

STRENGTH THROUGH PRAYER

"And it shall come to pass, that whosoever shall call on the name of the Lord shall be delivered." Joel 2:32

THINGS YOU WILL NEED
Three tumblers
A sheet of writing paper

EXPERIMENT
Lay the sheet of paper like a bridge across two of the tumblers. Place the third tumbler on the "bridge." The bridge collapses and the tumbler falls. At the appropriate time in the presentation, fold the paper accordian-style lengthwise. Again, place it across the tumblers and replace the third tumbler. This time, the reinforced paper will support the weight of the tumbler.

GOSPEL APPLICATION
While being persecuted by Amulon, the people of Alma prayed mightily to God for support. When Amulon commanded them to stop their cries to God, they continued to "pour out their hearts to him" (Mosiah 24:12). Because of their willingness to submit to the Lord, they were strengthened and were able to bear their burdens with ease (see Mosiah 24:15). When we feel the pressure of burdens (the tumbler) on our backs, we need to follow the prayerful example of Alma and his people. The Lord will strengthen us also (paper folding) if we are willing to "submit cheerfully and with patience to all the will of the Lord" (Mosiah 24:15).

ADDITIONAL APPLICATION
Strengthen Others—Luke 22:32 states, "and when thou art converted, strengthen thy brethren." This can happen in more

ways than one. If we learn a point of doctrine that helps our testimony grow, then we should share it with other Church members to strenghthen and uplift them. If we have new converts in our ward, we should strengthen them with continual love and support to help them become deeply rooted in the gospel. The other Church members and the new converts are represented by the unfolded piece of paper. Discuss ways to strengthen others in both situations as you fold the piece of paper.

STRENGTH THROUGH TRIALS

"Ye receive no witness until after the trial of your faith." Ether 12:6

THINGS YOU WILL NEED
Paper
Paper airplane-folding book (optional)

EXPERIMENT
Fold the paper into your favorite paper airplane as you give the lesson.

GOSPEL APPLICATION
"My people must be tried in all things," declares the Lord, "that they may be prepared to receive the glory that I have for them, even the glory of Zion; and he that will not bear chastisement is not worthy of my kingdom" (D&C 136:31). Facing trials and afflictions is one way the Lord strengthens us and helps us to prepare to receive His glory. Fold the paper into an airplane, with each fold representing a trial. You may even share a personal trial that has given you strength. Joseph Smith endured many trials throughout his life. While being held in the jail in Liberty, Missouri, he received these words of encouragement from the Lord: "My son, peace be unto thy soul; thine adversity and thine afflictions shall be but a small moment; And then, if thou endure it well, God shall exalt thee on high; thou shalt triumph over all thy foes" (D&C 121:7–8). Fly the airplane across the classroom to show that by enduring the "trials" (folds) the paper was given the strength needed to perform well.

STRENGTH TO ENDURE TRIALS

"The Lord will give strength unto his people." Psalm 29:11

THINGS YOU WILL NEED
Five uncooked eggs
Clay
Several books
Plastic bag (large enough to
cover one of the books)
Bowl

EXPERIMENT
Place the wide ends of four eggs upright into the clay, forming a square. If necessary, the extra egg can be broken into the bowl to prove to the class that the eggs are raw. Place the plastic bag over one of the books in case the eggs accidently break during the experiment. Stack the books one at a time on the four eggs until you have an impressive stack. Even though the eggs appear to be fragile, their shape makes them very strong.

GOSPEL APPLICATION
In Mosiah 24:8–22 we can read about the people of Alma who were in bondage to Amulon, the king of the Lamanites. During this time of great affliction, the people cried to the Lord for deliverance. The Lord did visit them in their afflictions and caused that their burdens should be light. They were strengthened and "did submit cheerfully and with patience to all the will of the Lord" (verse 15). In Psalm 29:11, the Lord promises to bless us with strength and peace. Demonstrate this by bringing attention to the stack of books and the fragile eggs. It may seem an impossible feat to stack the books on top of the

eggs without breaking them, but by carefully placing the books (starting with the plastic-covered book) one at a time on top of the eggs, it can be done. We, too, can be strengthened in our trials if we put our trust in the Lord.

ADDITIONAL APPLICATION

Sharing Burdens—When we are baptized, we covenant, among other things, to share one another's burdens (see Mosiah 18:8). Begin by placing only one egg on its side in the clay. As you stack the books (burdens) on top of the egg, it will eventually break under the weight of the books. Now place four eggs in the clay, each with the wide end down. The four eggs will be able to withstand greater weight as the books are stacked on top of them. When we support each other, we are strengthened and are able to handle a greater load.

THOUGHTS

"For as he thinketh in his heart, so is he." Proverbs 23:7

THINGS YOU WILL NEED
String with large nail tied to one end (could be any small, heavy object)

EXPERIMENT
Hold the string with the weight hanging below. Without moving your hand, think strongly about the weight moving in a circle. It will probably do so without visible movement of the hand. You can also think of it moving back and forth or side to side.

GOSPEL APPLICATION
Thoughts control our actions. Proverbs 23:7 states, "For as he thinketh in his heart, so is he." Before our actions are played out, they must begin as thoughts in our minds. Show the power of thought by presenting the experiment. Speaking of the consequences of uncontrolled thoughts, King Benjamin makes it clear when he states, "But this much I can tell you, that if ye do not watch yourselves, and your thoughts, and your words, and your deeds, and observe the commandments of God, and continue in the faith of what ye have heard concerning the coming of our Lord, even unto the end of your lives, ye must perish. And now, O man, remember, and perish not" (Mosiah 4:30). Although we place a good deal of emphasis on controlling bad thoughts, equal emphasis should be focused on the power of good thoughts. In order to reach our righteous goals, we must first see them in our minds.

TITHING

"And of all that thou shalt give me I will surely give the tenth unto thee." Genesis 28:22

THINGS YOU WILL NEED
One clear 9x13" baking dish (or similar)
Two clear pint-size jars
Large container of water with large opening
Medium container of water with medium opening
Eyedropper of water

EXPERIMENT
Label one of the jars "Myself" and one of the jars "The Lord." Place the two pint jars in the baking dish and display them on a table. At the appropriate times in the presentation, pour water from the containers into the jars.

GOSPEL APPLICATION
Malachi 3:10 states, "Bring ye all the tithes into the store-house, that there may be meat in mine house, and prove me now herewith, saith the Lord of hosts, if I will not open you the windows of heaven, and pour you out a blessing, that there shall not be room enough to receive it." What is our personal commitment to the law of tithing? Do we give it in small amounts—and grudgingly? Are we careful to give only what is required and nothing more? Or, do we give fully and willingly? Demonstrate these various attitudes toward tithing by using the eyedropper to represent one who gives grudgingly, the jar with a medium-sized opening to represent someone who gives just enough, and the jar with a large-sized opening someone who gives freely and willingly. With each container, pour some of the "tithing" into the Lord's jar. Now discuss with the class what

kind of blessings they would like to receive from the Lord. Do they want an eyedropperful of blessings? A medium amount of blessings? Or, do they want the blessings to overflow in their lives—so much that there will not be room enough to receive it? With each corresponding container, pour some of the blessings into the jar labeled "Myself." Finish by filling the jar to overflowing with the large container.

ADDITIONAL APPLICATION

Generosity—Deuteronomy 15:11 states, "Thou shalt open thine hand wide unto thy brother, to thy poor, and to thy needy, in thy land." For this demonstration you will need only one of the pint jars. Lable it "The Needy." Challenge the class to think about their attitude toward helping others. Are they represented by the eyedropper—one who complains and gives only a little? Are they represented by the jar with the medium-sized opening—giving only what they have to? Or, are they like the large jar—giving cheerfully and completely?

TRAPPED BY SIN

"The devil shall send forth his mighty winds, yea, his shafts in the whirlwind" Helaman 5:12

THINGS YOU WILL NEED
A marble
Clear glass jar

EXPERIMENT
Place the marble on the table, with the glass jar upside down over it. Make swirling motions with the jar, causing the marble to rotate also. Continue with the swirling motion of the jar as you lift it from the table. As long as you continue in this motion, the marble will continue to spin around the inside of the jar.

GOSPEL APPLICATION
In this experiment, we are represented by the marble. The glass jar represents the entrapments of Satan. We may be naive in recognizing his power. When he sends his whirlwinds of falsehoods we can get caught up in his lies, making it difficult to escape.

ADDITIONAL APPLICATION
Testimony—In order to maintain our testimonies we need to continually nourish them through scripture study, fasting, prayers, and service to others. When we fail to do these things, we are in danger of losing our testimonies. Demonstrate this by showing how the marble continues to stay in that jar as long as there is movement. When the movement stops, the marbles fall out.

TRIAL OF YOUR FAITH

"Ye receive no witness until after the trial of your faith." Ether 12:6

THINGS YOU WILL NEED
Raw milk (or heavy cream)
Small glass jar with tight-fitting lid
Salt (optional)
Bread or rolls (optional)

EXPERIMENT
Allow the milk or cream to sit in a warm place for 24–36 hours. Place in a sealed jar and shake vigorously until chunks of butter form. Pour off excess liquid and rinse with water. Add salt as needed. Spread butter on bread or roll and enjoy.

GOSPEL APPLICATION
Ether 12:6 teaches us that "ye receive no witness until after the trial of your faith." When faced with a trial, often we will not see the blessing until after the trial has passed. When we have completed the trial by exercising faith in Jesus Christ, then we can enjoy the resulting blessings. Demonstrate this by following the directions to make butter. Enjoy the "blessings" from the "trial" by spreading the butter on a piece of bread and eating it.

TRIBULATIONS

"Whosoever shall put their trust in God shall be supported in their trials . . . and shall be lifted up at the last day." Alma 36:3

THINGS YOU WILL NEED
Small clear jar with a lid
2 teaspoon metallic glitter
2 tablespoon sand
1 cup water
2 tablespoon oil

EXPERIMENT
Place the glitter and the sand in the jar. Add the water and the oil. Screw the lid tightly onto the jar and shake vigorously. Let everything settle. The glitter will float to the top of the water, while the sand settles to the bottom.

GOSPEL APPLICATION
As you shake the jar vigorously to represent trials, troubles, and afflictions, have someone read Alma 36:3. We learn from this verse that if we put our trust in God, we will be supported in our afflictions and be lifted up at the last day. After shaking the jar, set it down to demonstrate how the faithful (glitter) will be lifted up to receive glory, while the unfaithful (sand) will sink to the bottom. (See also D&C 58:2–4.)

ADDITIONAL APPLICATION
Faith—After putting the glitter, sand, water, and oil in the jar, screw the lid on securely and hold it up for the class to see. Tell the class that you will now separate the sand from the glitter without removing the lid and without using any special tools. Ask if anyone believes that your claim is possible. Many

will probably not believe, but encourage them to have faith and not dispute your claim. Have someone read Ether 12:6. Explain that many times, our faith will be tried and tested before we receive a witness (or an answer). Begin to shake the jar vigorously to symbolize the "trial of your faith." Set the jar on a table to demonstrate how the glitter separates from the sand—providing the "witness" for your claim.

TRUTH

"The truth of the Lord endureth for ever." Psalm 117:2

THINGS YOU WILL NEED
Clear drinking glass or jar with a flat bottom
Nickel, dime, or quarter
Small pitcher of water

EXPERIMENT
Allow the class to observe as you place the coin under the glass. It will look as if the coin is in the glass. As the class looks through the side of the glass at the coin, begin to fill the glass with water and watch how the coin seems to disappear.

GOSPEL APPLICATION
D&C 123:12 states, "For there are many yet on the earth among all sects, parties, and denominations, who are blinded by the subtle craftiness of men, whereby they lie in wait to deceive, and who are only kept from the truth because they know not where to find it." In our world today it is evident that the craftiness of men is trying to cover truth. But just because the world may say something contrary to God's truth and lead some to believe that God's laws have changed, it does not change the fact that "truth abideth forever and ever" (D&C 1:39).

TWO OR THREE WITNESSES

"In the mouth of two or three witnesses every word may be
established." Matthew 18:16

THINGS YOU WILL NEED
Large button
Two kitchen forks
Cup

EXPERIMENT
When you place the edge of the button on the rim of the
cup, it will fall off at once. When you place the forks on the
button as shown in the diagram, the button will balance on the
rim.

GOSPEL APPLICATION
In a court of law, witnesses help prove the truthfulness of a
story. It's hard to accept a story as truth if it can only be verified
by one person. In Matthew 18:16 the Lord says, "In the mouth
of two or three witnesses every word may be established." The
Lord followed through with these words when He brought
forth the Book of Mormon as another testament of Jesus
Christ. The Lord called for witnesses to testify of seeing the
gold plates that Joseph Smith translated. On its own, a story
may not be credible. With witnesses, it will be supported and
established. Demonstrate this by showing how the button falls
by itself but is supported with the help of the forks.

ADDITIONAL APPLICATION
Service to Others—The button in the demonstration
represents someone in need of help. Without support, they
continue to fall. We may be afraid to help, in fear that we may

fall also. D&C 6:33 states, "Fear not to do good, my sons, for whatsoever ye sow, that shall ye also reap; therefore, if ye sow good ye shall also reap good for your reward." We will receive blessings when we exercise courage and a willingness to help others. Demonstrate this by showing how the button can balance successfully with the help of the forks.

UNITED IN ALL THINGS

"Be determined in one mind and in one heart, united in all things." 2 Nephi 1:21

THINGS YOU WILL NEED

Two or more walnuts in shells

EXPERIMENT

It is difficult or impossible to crack a walnut by squeezing it in your hand. However, if you squeeze two walnuts together in your hand, one cracks easily.

GOSPEL APPLICATION

2 Nephi 1:21 states, "Be determined in one mind and in one heart, united in all things." Sometimes when we're working alone, it's hard to get a job done. In Ecclesiastes 4:9 we learn, "Two are better than one; because they have a good reward for their labour." When we unite with others to accomplish a common goal, we tend to have greater success.

ADDITIONAL APPLICATIONS

Book of Mormon—Using the Bible alone, it is hard to "crack" some of the mysteries of God. With the help of the Book of Mormon, we can break down some of these mysteries and have a better understanding of gospel principles.

Fellowshipping—Before we can "crack" the shell of someone we are trying to teach or fellowship, we need to find common ground, hobbies, or interests with the person. When we do this, we build relationships of trust and are then able to "crack" the barriers that surround them.

WELCOME OTHERS

"The stranger that dwelleth with you . . . thou shalt love him as thyself." Leviticus 19:34

THINGS YOU WILL NEED
Two bar magnets
Masking tape
Permanent marker
Stiff paper (optional)

EXPERIMENT
Prior to the experiment, place a piece of masking tape on each magnet (or cut two small people from stiff paper and attach one to each magnet). Label one magnet "Me," and the other magnet "New Member." Place the magnets on a flat surface. When brought close together, the two magnets will either attract or repel each other—depending on which ends of the magnets are brought together.

GOSPEL APPLICATION
When new members or visitors attend our Church meetings, we need to do our part in making them feel welcome. Mention several things that a new member or visitor could experience when they come to a meeting. If the experience makes a person feel welcome, place the magnets in a way where they attract each other. If the experience mentioned would repel a person, place the magnets in a way where they repel each other. Encourage the class members to always make others feel welcome through their words and actions.

ADDITIONAL APPLICATIONS
Attracting or Repelling Sin—Label one magnet "Me," and the other magnet "Sin." Do our thoughts, words, and actions

attract or repel sin? Discuss with the class various situations that would attract or repel sin. Position the magnets accordingly as you discuss each situation. The scriptures teach us that we should avoid even the very appearance of evil (1 Thessalonians 5:22). By doing so, we will repel sin and live a life that is worthy of blessings from our Heavenly Father.

Example—Label one magnet "My Example," and the other magnet "Nonmember." When we are baptized we promise to take upon us the name of Christ and follow the perfect example He set for us. Nonmembers will judge the Church according to the example we set. In Alma 39:11, we learn that Corianton's bad example kept the Zoramites from receiving the word of God when taught by Alma. Do our examples bring our friends closer to the Church, or do they push them away? Discuss possible situations that would either attract or discourage nonmembers from receiving the truth. Position the magnets accordingly as you discuss each situation.

ZEAL FOR RIGHTEOUSNESS

"But it is good to be zealously affected always in a good thing."
Galations 4:18

THINGS YOU WILL NEED
    Scissors
    Stiff paper
    Pen
    Balloon
    Wool cloth

EXPERIMENT
    Cut several people from the stiff paper using the pattern above as a guide. Lay the paper people on a table. Rub the balloon on the wool cloth, then hold the balloon about 4" above the paper people. They should jump up and down.

GOSPEL APPLICATION
    We learn in D&C 58:27 that "men should be anxiously engaged in a good cause, and do many things of their own free will, and bring to pass much righteousness." When we perform service or magnify our callings with enthusiasm, that enthusiasm can rub off on others. Our zeal for righteousness should show in everything we do. No matter what the activity, our positive attitude can help others get excited and involved. Demonstrate this by rubbing the balloon with the woolen cloth and holding it over the paper people to get them "excited."

ADDITIONAL APPLICATIONS
    Missionary Work—When Alma and Amulek went forth to preach the gospel, they were well received because "the Lord did pour out his Spirit on all the face of the land to prepare the

minds of the children of men, or to prepare their hearts to receive the word" (Alma 16:16). If we go forth to teach our friends the gospel without preparing them first through sincere fellowshipping, they may not receive the gospel message very well. Demonstrate this by holding the balloon over the paper people before you rub it with the wool cloth. Nothing happens. If we do our part and learn how to "rub" our friends in the right way and prepare them, they will be much more excited about the gospel message. Demonstrate this by rubbing the balloon with the wool cloth and holding the balloon over the paper people. They should be more "enthusiastic" now.

Activation—Demonstrate this experiment the same way as "Missionary Work" mentioned above, but explain that we need to learn how to "rub" the less-actives that we are responsible for in the right way so that they will once again become excited about the gospel.

INDEX

Soft answers, 127
Spiritual, differences, 129
    feast, 103
    gifts, 130
    nourishment, 132
    strength, 134
    warmth, 45
Spirituality, lack of, 67
Strength, spiritual, 134
    through prayer, 141
    through trials, 143
    to endure trials, 144
    in unity, 139
Strengthen, others, 141
    thy brethren, 50, 61
Strife, 96

T

Talents, sharing, 48, 118, 131
Temples, our bodies are, 82
Temptation, 7
    resisting, 109
Testimony, 35, 149
Thoughts, 146
Tithing, 95, 147
Trapped, by sin, 149
Trials, strength through, 143
    strength to endure, 144
    of your faith, 150
Treasures, hidden, 53
Tribulations, 151
Truth, 153

U

United, in all things, 156
Unity, strength in, 139
Unkind words, 43
Unspotted, from the world, 22

V

Virtue, 22

W

Warmth, spiritual, 45
Weaknesses, overcoming, 89
Welcome others, 157
Witnesses, two or three, 140, 154
Word of God, nourished by the, 79
Word of Wisdom, 53
Words, kind, 107
    unkind, 24, 43
Work, missionary, 159
Works, faith without, 119
    good, 124
World, overcoming the, 87

Z

Zeal, for righteousness, 159